MY FELT DOLL

MY FELT DOLL

SHELLY DOWN

EASY SEWING PATTERNS
FOR WONDERFULLY
WHIMSICAL DOLLS

David and Charles

www.stitchcraftcreate.co.uk

CONTENTS

Introduction

When I began making dolls a few years ago, I really didn't have much sewing experience at all. My Nan had taught me a few basic embroidery stitches when I was younger, but, to be honest, I thought that needlecrafts were best suited to little old ladies who spent their days drinking pots of tea and sorting embroidery threads! Oh, how very wrong I was...

Although my sewing skills were extremely limited when I started making dolls, I quickly noticed that my work improved dramatically with continued practise. Now, not only is it fun to create something by hand, it is also a very rewarding experience. I often find myself wondering just how many little stitches I've used to sew a doll when it's finished – each little stitch I've sewn is a tiny bit of love. It's such a wonderful feeling, knowing that I've created the entire doll from start to finish!

Vintage children's books, fairy tales and the cute, lovable style of Japanese Kawaii inspire many of my designs. Once I've come up with an idea for a doll or toy, I make a basic sketch of the design into my notebook. Then I break down every aspect of the sketch to create the pattern pieces, which I draw onto graph paper. Usually, I need to make and re-make pattern pieces many times before I'm satisfied with the results, but the process is certainly worth the effort once everything comes together!

I feel it's very important for me to write the instructions for my patterns in a very simple, easy-to-follow manner, so even a beginner sewer can feel confident in his or her abilities to make something wonderful. It is very rewarding to make something by hand, especially if it is fun and easy to make. And it's my hope to inspire more people to dust off their scissors and pincushions to give sewing a try!

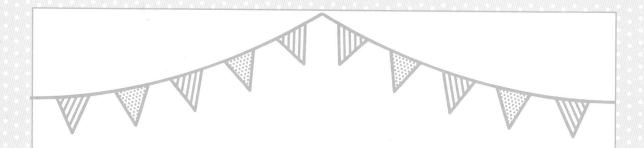

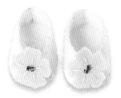

HOW THIS
BOOK WORKS

First, I've created a sweet, lovable little basic doll (see How to Sew the Basic Doll), which is designed to be sewn by hand in felt. This basic doll pattern is the same for all the projects throughout the book, with the exception of a few changes to facial features and hairstyles. Then you'll find a collection of 11 projects to make an outfit, each based on a specific theme such as a schoolgirl, a little princess, a beach babe and so on. I have designed these projects with simple, easy-to-follow instructions, patterns and illustrations, so even a beginner sewer will enjoy making them.

I've used a variety of different felt types to make the dolls and outfits, which include handwoven wool felt, pure wool felt, wool blend felt and synthetic felts (see Felt). All the seams are sewn by hand with embroidery thread (floss), using stitches from the Stitch Guide (see Stitch Guide) at the end of the book. There is no need for you to add a seam allowance or to turn the pieces inside out after sewing, as each piece is sewn with the right side of the felt on the outside. The finished dolls measure about 25cm (10in) tall, perfect for a little one to tuck into his or her pocket and take along on all their adventures!

FELT

FELT IS AN AMAZING TEXTILE! IT'S EASY TO WORK WITH, AND, UNLIKE MOST FABRICS, THE EDGES WILL NOT UNRAVEL OR FRAY ONCE THEY ARE CUT. TRADITIONALLY, FELT IS MADE BY MATTING AND CONDENSING WOOL (YARN) FIBRES TOGETHER, A PROCEDURE THAT CREATES A WONDERFULLY VERSATILE FABRIC, PERFECT FOR DOLL MAKING. IT CAN ALSO BE MADE BY BLENDING OTHER FIBRES WITH WOOL, OR BY USING JUST SYNTHETIC OR ACRYLIC FIBRES.

WHILE THERE ARE MANY DIFFERENT VARIETIES OF FELTS, I RECOMMEND THAT YOU CHOOSE A GOOD QUALITY WOOL OR WOOL BLEND FELT TO MAKE THE MAIN BODIES OF THE DOLLS IN THIS BOOK. THE HIGHER QUALITY FELTS, WHICH ARE MADE WITH WOOL, ARE MORE DURABLE AND HOLD UP BETTER TO USE AND HANDLING THAN SYNTHETIC OR ACRYLIC FELTS. TO HELP YOU FAMILIARIZE YOURSELF WITH THIS WONDERFUL MATERIAL, I HAVE LISTED BELOW SOME EXAMPLES OF THE DIFFERENT TYPES OF FELT THAT ARE AVAILABLE ON THE MARKET.

PURE WOOL FELT

Usually made from the wool that lies closest to the sheep's skin, pure wool felt is buttery soft, cuts cleanly and sews up beautifully. It is much stronger and denser than other types of felt and is less likely to pill, rip at the seams or to stretch, and as wool is naturally flame and water resistant and doesn't fray, this type of felt has these qualities, too. Pure wool felt can be purchased in a wide variety of vibrant colours.

WOOL BLEND FELT

Most often, wool blend felts are made from a blend of wool and rayon, the latter of which is made from purified cellulose, primarily sourced from wood pulp. Its properties are very similar to linen or cotton, which makes it perfect for blending with other fabrics. Wool blend felts are very similar to pure wool felt, as they are soft and durable, less likely to pill and are easy to cut out and sew. And like pure wool felts, wool blend felts retain their shape well, do not fray and can be used in a variety of crafts.

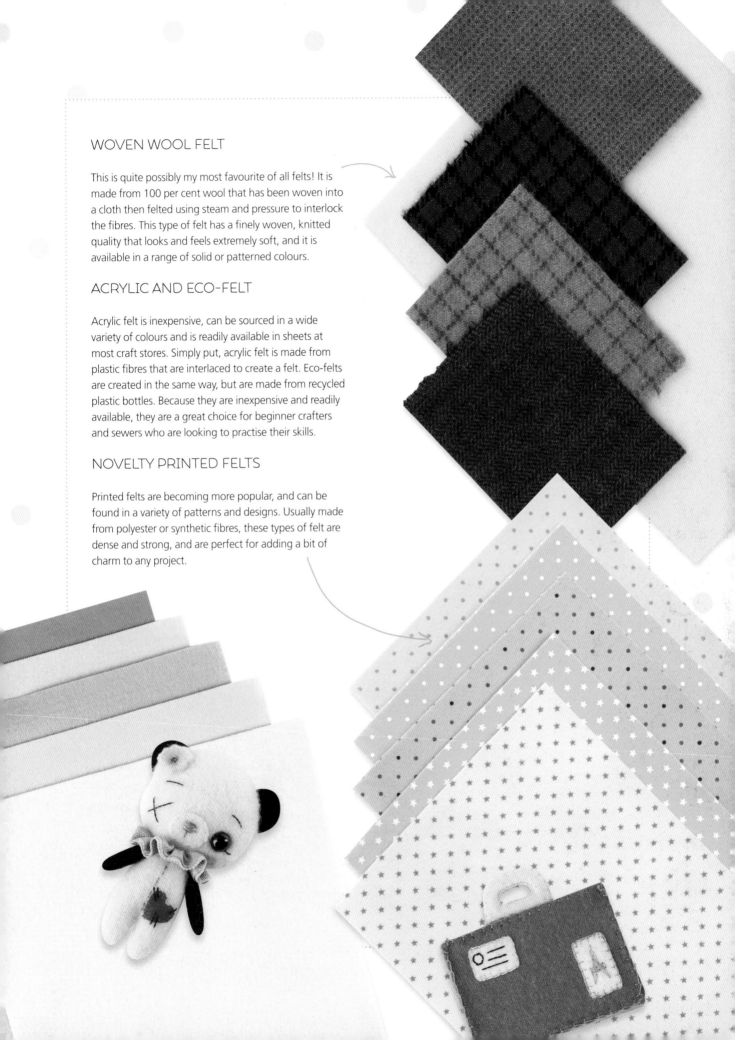

WOVEN WOOL FELT

This is quite possibly my most favourite of all felts! It is made from 100 per cent wool that has been woven into a cloth then felted using steam and pressure to interlock the fibres. This type of felt has a finely woven, knitted quality that looks and feels extremely soft, and it is available in a range of solid or patterned colours.

ACRYLIC AND ECO-FELT

Acrylic felt is inexpensive, can be sourced in a wide variety of colours and is readily available in sheets at most craft stores. Simply put, acrylic felt is made from plastic fibres that are interlaced to create a felt. Eco-felts are created in the same way, but are made from recycled plastic bottles. Because they are inexpensive and readily available, they are a great choice for beginner crafters and sewers who are looking to practise their skills.

NOVELTY PRINTED FELTS

Printed felts are becoming more popular, and can be found in a variety of patterns and designs. Usually made from polyester or synthetic fibres, these types of felt are dense and strong, and are perfect for adding a bit of charm to any project.

OTHER ESSENTIAL MATERIALS

YOU'LL NEED A FEW BASIC SEWING TOOLS AND NOTIONS FOR MAKING THE DOLLS AND THEIR OUTFITS, WHICH I HAVE LISTED BELOW. AS A BASIC KIT TO GET STARTED, YOU'LL NEED A SHARP PAIR OF DRESSMAKING SCISSORS AND A PAIR OF EMBROIDERY SCISSORS, PINS AND SEWING NEEDLES, A FEW SHEETS OF FELT, EMBROIDERY THREAD (FLOSS), A DISAPPEARING INK MARKER, A RULER AND SOME STUFFING. YOU SHOULD BE ABLE TO SOURCE ALL OF THESE AT YOUR LOCAL FABRIC OR CRAFT STORE, AND YOU CAN ADD TO THIS KIT AS YOUR FELTING SKILLS DEVELOP. ANY OCCASIONALLY USED ITEMS NEEDED TO COMPLETE SPECIFIC PROJECTS ARE LISTED WITHIN THE 'YOU WILL NEED' LISTS AT THE BEGINNING OF EACH PROJECT, SO MAKE SURE YOU READ THESE CAREFULLY BEFORE YOU BEGIN CUTTING AND STITCHING.

WOOL (YARN) (1)

This is used for making hair, and I think one of the hardest parts of making these felt dolls is choosing which wool to use – not only are there so many different types of yarn, but there is also an array of colours available to suit your taste. You can actually use any type of wool for your dolls' hair, so become creative and have fun with the texture and colour! Below I've listed a few examples of the wools I've used for the projects.

Mohair wool Made from the hair of angora goats, this is one of the oldest textile fibres known. Silky and soft, it is a dream to work with and comes in many different varieties that include brushed mohair or bouclé, which has a characteristic curly appearance.

Icelandic wool Made from the fleece of Icelandic sheep, this is a fairly coarse wool, but it's one of my favourites because of its lovely wavy texture. It is

perfect for making doll hair – I personally prefer the Lett-Lopi Lite for doing this.

Wool blends Many different wool blend yarns are available, ranging from natural to acrylic fibres.

EMBROIDERY THREAD (FLOSS) (2)

Most needlecraft stores sell embroidery thread and it is available in a rainbow of different colours. I'm partial to DMC cotton embroidery floss, as it is a soft thread made from 100 per cent Egyptian cotton. Because it has been double mercerized, it has a brilliant sheen and is suitable for using on all types of fabric.

Each skein is comprised of six strands, which are easily separated so you can adjust the thickness of your stitching simply by adjusting the number of strands. For the projects in this book, just one strand of thread is needed for sewing up all the seams and for adding facial features.

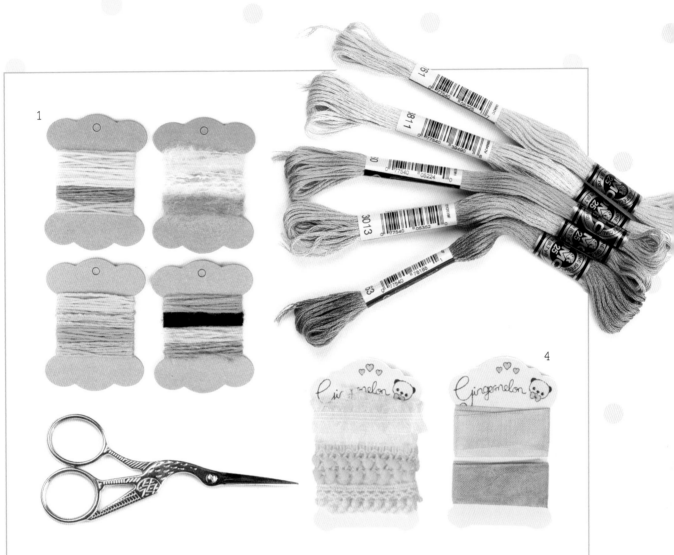

EMBROIDERY SCISSORS (3)

Classic embroidery scissors feature slender blades and a strong frame, making them ideal for cutting out smaller pieces of felt and snipping threads.

DRESSMAKING SCISSORS

Because felt is a fairly dense fabric it tends to be a little harder to cut, which in turn can eventually cause a pair of scissors to become dull. So if you're able, invest in a pair of good quality dressmaking scissors. Not only do they cut felt like butter, but they also retain their sharpness much longer and are well worth the extra expense!

SEWING PINS AND NEEDLES

It's very important to use pins and needles with sharp tips, because blunt pins may leave holes in your fabric that don't easily disappear. I prefer to use thinner pins and needles for my dollmaking, as they're easier to insert into the dense felt fabric.

LONG DOLL NEEDLE

This is an extra long, strong needle mostly used for attaching dolls' arms to their bodies, and it can be found at fabric and craft stores.

TRIM (4)

There are many different types and colours of trim available, and they are used to add detail to the dolls' outfits. In these projects I've mostly used narrow cotton lace, tiny pom-pom trim and narrow elasticized sheer lace to achieve a dainty look.

FRAY CHECK LIQUID

Fray Check liquid is a type of clear drying glue used to prevent fabric from fraying at the edges, which can

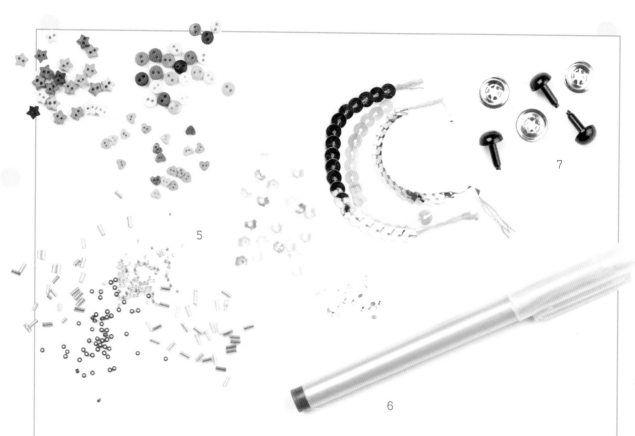

5

6

7

usually be found at fabric stores. Run a small bead of Fray Check along the cut edge of fabric, ribbon, lace trim or seam binding to prevent it from fraying.

SEED BEADS, SEQUINS AND GLITTER (5)

Widely available in many colours and finishes, these little notions are wonderful for adding detail to your projects. As for glitter, it's shimmery, bright and sparkly – what more can I say?

DISAPPEARING INK MARKER (6)

This is a non-permanent ink pen, usually with blue or purple ink, which is used to transfer markings onto fabric. The ink vanishes over time, but it can be made to disappear faster on the slightest contact with water. So once you have completed a project, use a cotton bud (Q-tip) soaked in water to lightly dab any area that still has markings on it — the ink will instantly darken, but as it dries it will completely disappear.

SAFETY EYES AND CONNECTORS (7)

Safety eyes, or craft eyes, are available in different sizes and colours, and are used mainly for handmade plush toys and amigurumi. They consist of two parts: a plastic front (eye) with a smooth straight or threaded post; then a plastic or metal washer that fits onto the back of the post. I've used black safety eyes, 10.5mm (⅝in) diameter, with straight posts and metal washers throughout this book, but you may want to consider using coloured eyes to customize your dolls.

HAIR CLIPS AND CLAMPS

Small hair clips and clamps are a fun way to add some style to your dolls' hair and can be found at many supermarkets or pharmacies in a wide range of sizes and colours. Tiny metal clips can be decorated with pretty felt flower accessories that are easily stitched onto the prongs of the clip.

SNAP CLOSURES

Snap closures, also known as press studs, pops, snaps or tich, are used for fastening clothing. They consist of a pair of interlocking discs, made out of metal or plastic, which, when closed, stay locked together until a certain amount of force is applied to open them. The female side of the disc has an indent while the male side has a raised nub.

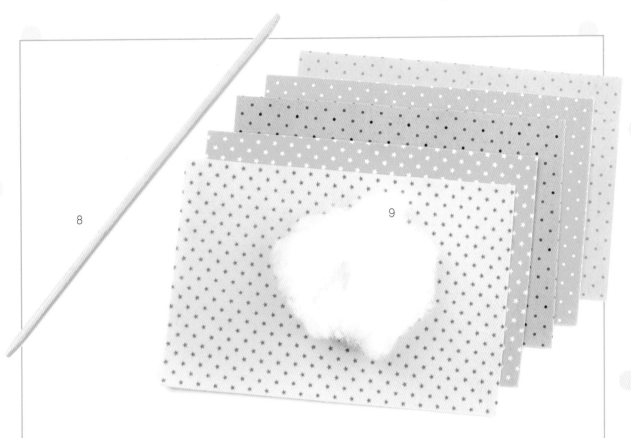

8

9

HOOK AND EYE CLOSURES

Another method of fastening clothing together, these consist of a metal hook made of flattened wire bent into a hook shape, and an eye of the same material into which the hook fits.

CLEAR-DRYING CRAFT GLUE

You will need some of this to attach the hair to the dolls' heads and to create their hairstyles, as well as to adhere glitter to felt.

RULER AND PENCIL

You'll need an ordinary ruler and pencil, because they will be useful for connecting grid lines as you prepare certain pattern pieces for sewing.

WOODEN SPOON AND COCKTAIL (ORANGE) STICK (8)

These will be your stuffing tools: use the wooden spoon to help push stuffing into larger areas, while the cocktail stick is perfect for stuffing smaller ones.

STUFFING (9)

Many types of stuffing are available from craft stores, ranging from natural to synthetic fibres. I prefer to use a supreme polyester fibre fill, as it's lovely and soft, and also holds its shape well.

AWL AND WIRE CUTTERS

These are both optional, but the awl is handy for piercing holes in the dolls' faces for the safety eyes, while the wire cutters can come in extremely useful for trimming back the posts of safety eyes once they've been inserted into the felt.

PAPER

Trace the pattern pieces from the book onto computer printer paper before cutting them out. Please be sure to label the pattern pieces with the corresponding labels so that you can keep them organized.

HOW TO SEW

THE BASIC DOLL

THE
Basic Doll

ALL THE SWEET LITTLE FELT DOLLS IN THIS BOOK ARE MADE FROM THE SAME BASIC PATTERN SHOWN HERE, WITH THE EXCEPTION OF THE LITTLE MERMAID DOLL THAT HAS A TAIL INSTEAD OF LEGS. I'VE USED A COMBINATION OF 100 PER CENT MERINO WOOL FELT AND MERINO WOOL BLEND FELTS TO MAKE THIS BASIC DOLL, WHICH IS COMPLETELY HAND SEWN USING EMBROIDERY THREAD (FLOSS) AND STITCHES FROM THE STITCH GUIDE (SEE STITCH GUIDE). I'VE KEPT THINGS NICE AND EASY, SO THERE IS NO NEED FOR YOU TO ADD A SEAM ALLOWANCE OR TO REMEMBER TO TURN THE PIECES INSIDE OUT AFTER SEWING, AS EACH IS SEWN WITH THE WRONG SIDES TOGETHER. THIS FINISHED DOLL IS THE PERFECT SIZE FOR ANY LITTLE ONE TO BRING ALONG ON AN ADVENTURE!

YOU WILL Need

- DRESSMAKING SCISSORS • EMBROIDERY SCISSORS • PINS • NEEDLES • LONG DOLL NEEDLE
- DISAPPEARING INK MARKER • PINK COLOURED PENCIL OR POWDER BLUSH
- CLEAR-DRYING CRAFT GLUE • RULER • COTTON BUD (Q-TIP) • WOODEN SPOON
- COCKTAIL (ORANGE) STICK OR CHOPSTICK • PAPER FOR PATTERN CUTTING
- SHOE-BOX LID • OPTIONAL: AWL, WIRE CUTTERS

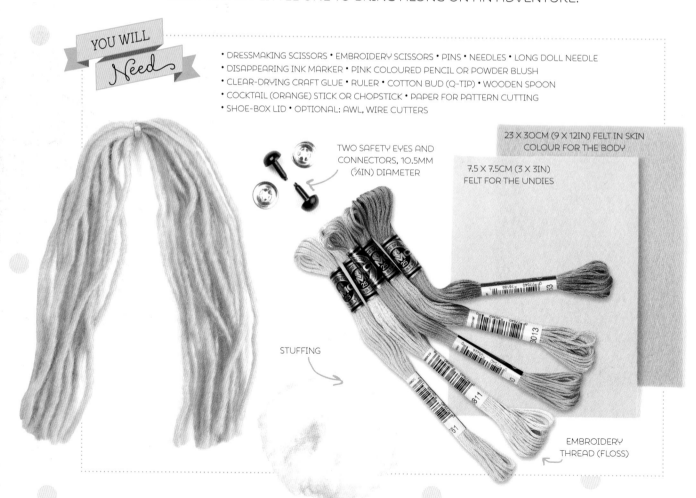

TWO SAFETY EYES AND CONNECTORS, 10.5MM (⅜IN) DIAMETER

23 X 30CM (9 X 12IN) FELT IN SKIN COLOUR FOR THE BODY

7.5 X 7.5CM (3 X 3IN) FELT FOR THE UNDIES

STUFFING

EMBROIDERY THREAD (FLOSS)

LAYOUT AND CUTTING

1 Make a photocopy or trace the pattern pieces for the basic doll and your project onto paper. Then cut out the pattern pieces and pin each one onto your chosen felts.

2 Carefully cut around the patterns, using your dressmaking scissors to cut out the larger pieces and embroidery scissors to cut out the smaller ones.

3 To mark the grid on the doll's face, keep the head pattern piece pinned in place and gently lift its outer edges, using your disappearing ink marker to mark the beginning of the lines onto the felt. Then remove the pattern piece and use the ruler to connect the lines, which will guide the eye, nose and mouth placement in later steps.

4 Finally, add the line at the ankle on your leg pieces with your disappearing ink marker.

HEAD

1 With your disappearing ink marker, transfer the facial markings shown on the pattern onto the piece of felt you have cut out for the face, using your pattern piece as a guide.

2 Embroider the nose and mouth onto the face, using stem stitch (see Stitch Guide).

3 Being very careful, use the tip of the embroidery scissors or an awl to make two tiny holes for the eyes at the centre of the X (see **Fig A**), where the vertical and horizontal lines meet.

4 Insert safety eyes with connectors at the back, making sure you slide the connector firmly down onto each post as far as it will go (see **Fig A**). Optional: once you've connected the eye parts, trim back the plastic posts of the safety eyes with your wire cutters to leave about 4mm (⅛in) of post beyond the connectors.

A

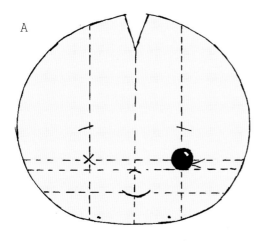

5 Using straight stitches (see Stitch Guide), embroider the eyelashes at the outer corners of the eyes with the eyebrows just above them. Also add a bit of rosy colour to the cheeks with your pink coloured pencil or powder blush.

6 Now fold the front and back pieces of the head vertically in half, wrong sides facing, and whip stitch (see Stitch Guide) the tiny cut-out V-shaped darts on each piece together. Doing this will help to give the finished head a more rounded appearance.

ASSEMBLING THE HEAD

1 Place the felt head front onto the head back, wrong sides facing, and pin together. Starting at A at the bottom of the head, blanket stitch (see Stitch Guide) all the way around until you reach B (see **Fig B**). Do not end off your thread (floss).

2 Add stuffing to the head, using the wooden spoon to gently push the stuffing up inside. Continue to fill out the face and as you near the opening, use your narrower cocktail (orange) stick or a chopstick to gently push the stuffing into the cheek areas (see **Fig B**).

B

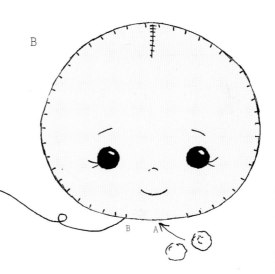

3 As you fill nearer the opening at the bottom, start blanket stitching the opening closed, adding more stuffing as you go, and round out the chin area before you finally close the hole. The face should now be fully rounded and quite firm, but not to the point of bursting at the seams.

BODY

1 Position the front of the body onto the back of the body, wrong sides facing. Then whip stitch around the entire body, starting at the left side of the neck and stitching all the way around to the area where the shoulder meets the neck at the opposite side (see **Fig C**).

2 Now add stuffing, using the wooden spoon to push the stuffing down inside the body. Continue adding more until you reach the shoulder area then use your cocktail stick or chopstick to push stuffing into this area (see **Fig C**).

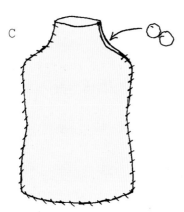

3 Continue whip stitching up the opposite side of the neck then end off your thread, but do not cut it. Add more stuffing to fill up the neck area.

4 Run a tiny gathering stitch (see Stitch Guide) just below the top edge of the neck to pull together the pieces of fabric. Gently tighten the thread to close the hole, adding more stuffing as you go to plump up the neck area. It's best to stuff the neck area as firmly as possible to provide a good base for supporting the head (see **Fig D**).

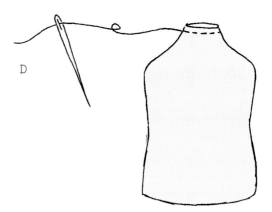

5 Once you've closed the hole, hand stitch the top area completely closed so you end up with a tight, rounded nub. Keep the thread attached to use later when attaching the head to the body (see **Fig E**).

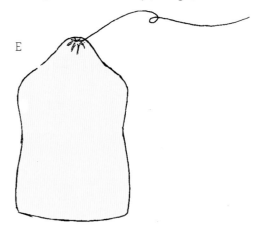

ARMS

1 Taking the two pieces of felt you cut for one arm, place them together, wrong sides facing. Then whip stitch around the pair, leaving an opening at the back of the arm for the stuffing (see **Fig F**).

2 Now add small bits of the stuffing to the arm, using your cocktail stick to gently push this up into the upper arm and down into the hand area. Keep adding little bits of stuffing until the entire arm is full then, whip stitch the opening closed (see **Fig F**).

3 Repeat Steps 1 to 2 to assemble the other arm.

F

LEGS

1 Pin the two pieces of felt you cut for one of these together, wrong sides facing. Then whip stitch around the entire leg, starting at A and working your way around to B (see **Fig G**), but do not end off your thread yet.

2 Add small pinches of stuffing to the foot, filling the area firmly right up to the line you marked at the ankle area. Insert a pin horizontally at that line, taking it all the way through to the back of the foot and out again through the front (see **Fig G**). Now add a few more pinches of stuffing to fill up the calf area.

3 Insert a threaded needle into the centre area of the marked line at the ankle and out through the side seam (see **Fig G**).

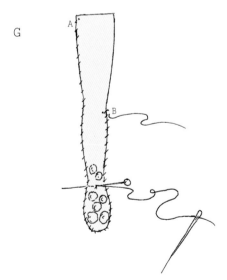

G

4 Now bend the foot at a 90-degree angle. Keeping the foot bent the entire time, use the thread to ladder stitch (see Stitch Guide) the foot to the lower leg where the top of the foot meets the bottom of the leg. Once

you reach the opposite side, remove the pin and repeat the ladder stitch across the seam again to create a sturdy join that should hold its shape well. Then end off the thread (see **Fig H**).

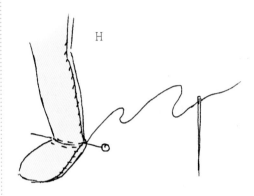

H

5 Now use your cocktail stick to push some stuffing down into the heel area of each foot.

6 Continue to whip stitch from where you left off at B, working your way up to C (see **Fig I**). Tie off your thread, but do not cut it yet.

7 Add stuffing to fill up the rest of each leg, stopping about 5mm (¼in) below the top edge. Then blanket stitch the top of the leg closed (see **Fig I**).

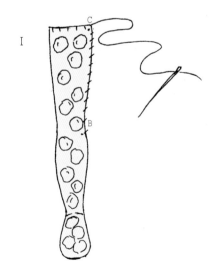

I

8 Repeat Steps 1 to 7 to assemble the other leg.

ATTACHING THE HEAD TO THE BODY

1 Position the head on the neck, centering it and matching the seams on either side of the head with the seams on either side of the neck.

2 Pin the head to the neck by inserting two pins into chest at the front and up into the head. Turn the doll around, so that the back of the doll is facing you. Now insert two pins up through her back and into the back of the head.

3 Turn your doll around again so that she's facing you. Using the strand of embroidery thread you kept attached from the neck area of the body, start ladder stitching around the head and neck, beginning at the right side of the neck. Work your way around the front of the head and neck to the opposite seam on the left, and then around the back of the head, returning to where you began (see **Fig J**).

4 You'll find that the head is still a bit wobbly, so work around in the same way a few more times to anchor the head firmly onto the neck. Each time you work around, take the ladder stitch a teeny bit lower down the neck and a teeny bit higher on the face, about 1 to 2mm (⅛ to ¹⁄₃₂in) each time. This will attach the head closer to the neck so it is a lot more stable.

5 It's very important to keep your ladder stitches very tiny and straight as you work around, as this will give a nice finish to the seam. Gently pull the thread every now and then as you stitch around to make the stitches disappear, but don't pull too tightly as this may pucker the seam.

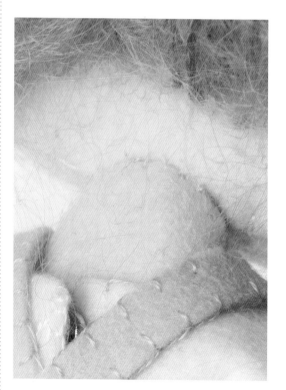

J

ATTACHING THE ARMS AND
LEGS TO THE BODY

1 Pin the arms to the sides of body. Using your long doll needle threaded with two strands of embroidery thread, insert the needle underneath one of the arms into the seam on the body where the arm will be located. Pass it through the body and straight out through the other arm area on the opposite side.

2 Insert the needle into the second arm, imagining that you are sewing two-holed buttons on at the top of each arm. Now pass the needle through the body again and out through the original arm in the same manner, repeating the process a few more times. Then end off underneath one arm (see **Fig K**).

3 Pin the legs to the bottom seam of the body and ladder stitch the front and back of each leg onto the seam (see **Fig L**).

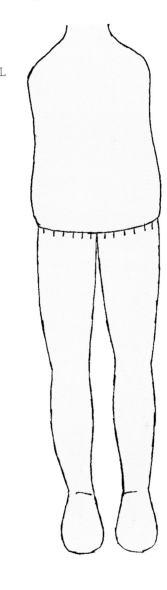

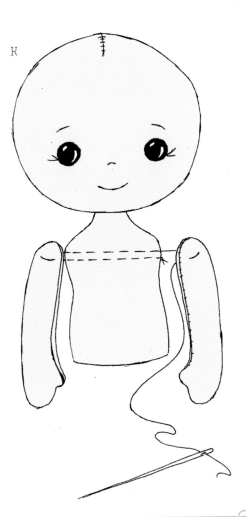

HAIR

1 To start making the hair, wrap your chosen wool (yarn) around a shoebox lid. For my doll I created approximately 66 strands once the ends were cut, each measuring about 50cm (20in) in length (see **Fig M**).

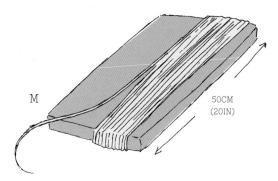

M

50CM
(20IN)

2 Carefully slide the wool from the box, keeping all the strands even. With a piece of wool in a contrasting colour, tie the centre of the bundle together but don't make a knot. Cut the loops at each end of the bundle so that the hair is straight at either end.

3 Position the bundle of wool directly onto the head seam, centering it in the middle of the seam. Pin this in place (see **Fig N**).

N

4 To attach the bundle onto the head, double thread a needle with embroidery thread to match the hair colour. Insert the needle through the back of the head beneath the bundle, just below the head seam. Bring it out through the front of the head under the bundle, directly below the head seam, pulling the thread tightly as you go. Then remove the contrasting wool tie from the centre of the bundle.

5 Repeat Step 4 several times to secure the bundle onto the head seam. Then end off the thread at the back of the head.

6 Gather all the hair and move it up and out of the way. Apply a layer of craft glue to the back of the head with a clean cotton bud (Q-tip), spreading this evenly to coat the entire area (see **Fig O**).

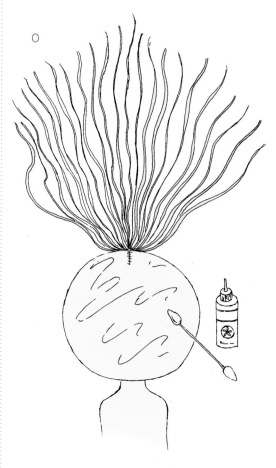

O

8 Using a cotton bud, gently push each strand of hair down into the glue and allow it to dry.

9 Spread a thin line of glue just in front of the seams on either side of the face at the front and cover each side with one or two of strands of wool. Allow all this to dry thoroughly.

10 Finally trim the ends of the hair and cut a fringe in front if desired (see **Fig Q**).

7 Now carefully place individual strands of wool onto the glued area, so that one layer of strands completely covers the back of the head. Make sure each strand is even and straight, from the top of the head down to the base. The strands of hair left over at the top of the bundle will be used later to cover the bottom layer once the glue has completely dried (see **Fig P**).

P

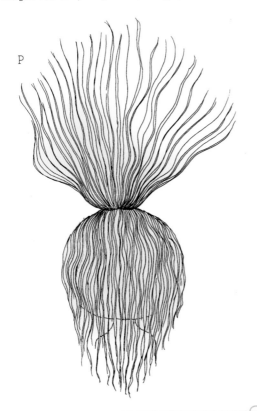

UNDIES

1 Using a contrasting embroidery thread and the lazy daisy stitch (see Stitch Guide), stitch a little flower onto the front of the felt piece you have cut out for the undies.

2 Fold the undies in half at the crotch, wrong sides facing, and whip stitch the sides together in a thread that matches the colour of the undies.

3 Blanket stitch around the waistband and leg openings with your contrasting embroidery thread. The blanket stitch will reinforce the openings and prevent them from warping while you dress them on the doll.

PATTERNS
Basic Doll

All the patterns are actual size, so there is no need to enlarge or reduce them.

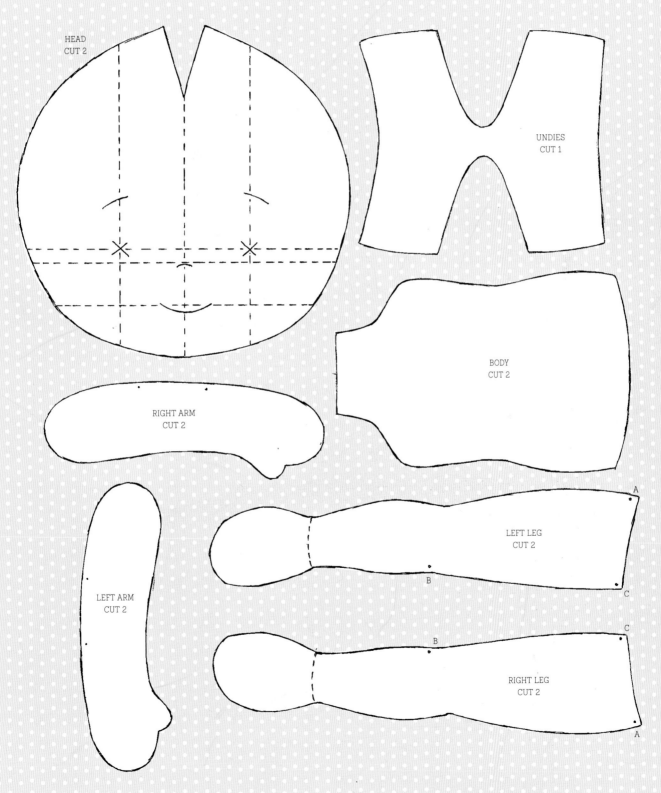

HEAD
CUT 2

UNDIES
CUT 1

BODY
CUT 2

RIGHT ARM
CUT 2

LEFT ARM
CUT 2

LEFT LEG
CUT 2

A

B

C

RIGHT LEG
CUT 2

C

B

A

LITTLE
Mermaid

THE ENCHANTING MERMAID IN THIS PROJECT WAS INSPIRED BY TALES OF THE BEAUTIFUL MYTHICAL CREATURES OF THE SEA. SHE WEARS AN EMBROIDERED SEASHELL BIKINI TOP THAT CLOSES AT THE BACK WITH A TINY SNAP, AND THERE ARE A FEW VARIATIONS FOR EMBELLISHING HER TAIL – YOU CAN KEEP IT PLAIN, SEW ON SEQUINS WITH SEED BEADS AT THE CENTRE AND/OR EMBELLISH THE FIN WITH FANCY EMBROIDERY STITCHES AND SEED BEADS. I'VE CHOSEN A BEAUTIFUL BRUSHED SURI ALPACA WOOL (YARN) FOR THE HAIR TO ACHIEVE A SOFT, FLOATY LOOK.

YOU WILL *Need*

- MATERIALS FOR THE BASIC DOLL PROJECT (SEE HOW TO SEW THE BASIC DOLL)
- BEADING NEEDLE
- SMALL SNAP CLOSURE, 5MM (¼IN) DIAMETER
- TINY METAL HAIR CLIP, 2CM (¾IN) LENGTH

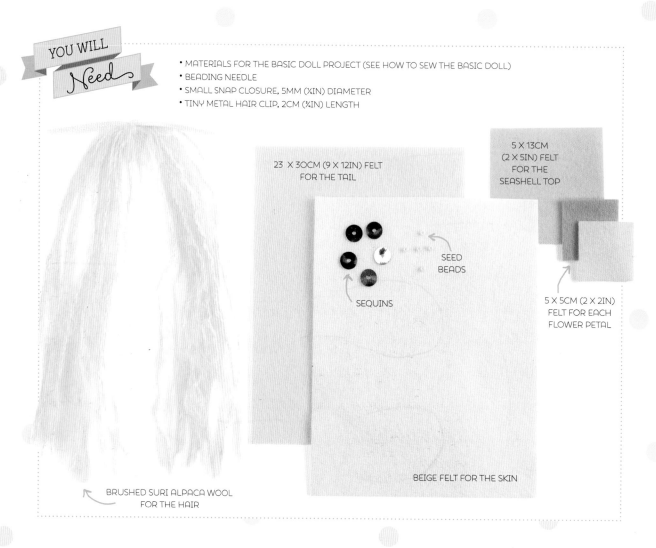

23 X 30CM (9 X 12IN) FELT FOR THE TAIL

5 X 13CM (2 X 5IN) FELT FOR THE SEASHELL TOP

SEED BEADS

SEQUINS

5 X 5CM (2 X 2IN) FELT FOR EACH FLOWER PETAL

BEIGE FELT FOR THE SKIN

BRUSHED SURI ALPACA WOOL FOR THE HAIR

LAYOUT AND CUTTING

1 Follow Steps 1 to 4 of the Layout and Cutting section from the Basic Doll project (see How to Sew the Basic Doll).

HEAD

1 Follow Steps 1 to 6 of the Head section from the Basic Doll project (see How to Sew the Basic Doll).

ASSEMBLING THE HEAD

1 Follow Steps 1 to 3 of the Assembling the Head section from the Basic Doll project (see How to Sew the Basic Doll).

BODY AND TAIL

1 Using your disappearing ink marker, transfer the dotted line indicated on the pattern of the body onto both your body felt pieces. These will be your guides for positioning the waistband of the mermaid's tail.

2 If you'd like to add sequins and/or embroidered details to the tail and fin, transfer the sequin placement markings shown on the tail pattern onto the front tail felt piece, as you did with the face grid (see How to Sew the Basic Doll).

3 Lay the front tail piece onto the front body piece, aligning the top of the tail's waist with the dotted line that you drew on the body in Step 1. Then appliqué stitch (see Stitch Guide) the waistband of the tail onto the body.

4 Repeat Step 3 with the back tail and body piece, making sure you reverse the pieces first.

5 For the doll's belly button, embroider a tiny lazy daisy flower (see Stitch Guide) on the front of the body, just above the waistband of the tail.

6 Attach a sequin with a seed bead at each point where the diagonal lines you drew in Step 2 meet on the tail. Embroider the fin with small running stitches (see Stitch Guide) directly onto the drawn lines and sew seed beads onto the marked dots (see **Fig A**).

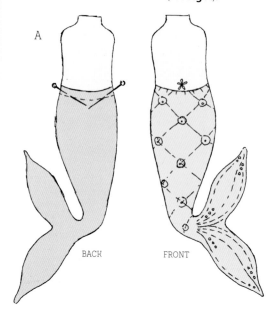

A

BACK   FRONT

ASSEMBLING THE BODY AND TAIL

1 Pin the front body to the back body, wrong sides facing. Using a matching embroidery thread (floss), whip stitch (see Stitch Guide) down one side of the body. Start at one side of the neck and work down until you reach the waistband. End off your thread.

2 Starting at A on the waistband of the tail and using matching embroidery thread, whip stitch around to B but do not end off your thread (see **Fig B**). Add tiny pinches of stuffing to fill up the first fin.

3 Continue whip stitching around to C then fill the second fin with stuffing. Now continue stitching and filling up the tail in this manner until you reach the opposite side of the waistband and end off your thread (see **Fig B**).

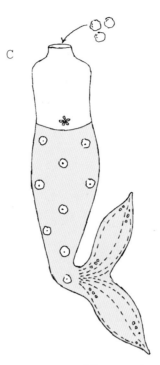

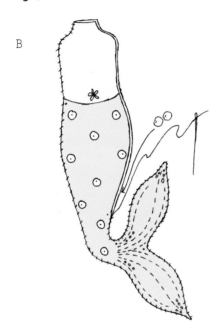

4 Change your thread to one that matches the body colour and continue stitching up to the area where the shoulder meets the neck on the opposite side.

5 Add stuffing through the gap in the neck, using the wooden spoon to push filling down inside the body and tail. Continue adding more until the stuffing reaches the shoulder area then use your cocktail (orange) stick or chopstick to push stuffing into this (see **Fig C**).

6 To complete this stage, follow Steps 3 to 5 from the Body section of the Basic Doll project (see How to Sew the Basic Doll).

ARMS

1 Follow Steps 1 to 3 of the Arms section from the Basic Doll project (see How to Sew the Basic Doll).

ATTACHING THE HEAD TO THE BODY

1 Follow Steps 1 to 5 of the Attaching the Head to the Body section from the Basic Doll project (see How to Sew the Basic Doll).

ATTACHING THE ARMS TO THE BODY

1 Follow Steps 1 to 2 of the Attaching the Arms and Legs to the Body section from the Basic Doll project (see How to Sew the Basic Doll).

HAIR

1 Follow Steps 1 to 10 of the Hair section from the Basic Doll project (see How to Sew the Basic Doll).

SEASHELL TOP

1 Using the disappearing ink marker, transfer the line markings from each shell pattern onto your felt pieces.

2 Embroider each shell pattern onto the seashell top using lazy daisy stitch then blanket stitch (see Stitch Guide) around the outline of each shell.

3 Fit the top onto the doll to determine where to attach the snap closure, then sew this in place at the back of the top (see **Fig D**).

D

FLOWER PETAL HAIR ACCESSORY

1 Using the disappearing ink marker, transfer the line markings from the petal pattern onto the piece of felt that will be your top flower. Then use a contrasting embroidery thread colour to stitch these lines onto the flower, but do not end off your thread.

2 Place the second flower petal felt piece behind the first, arranging it so that the petals of the second flower are slightly off-centre from the first. Insert a threaded needle in through the back of both petals and out through the centre of the front petal (see **Fig E**).

E

3 Stitch seed beads onto the centre of the top flower petal. Then take the thread through to the back of the flower and position the flower on the hair clip, so that it is centred on top. Now sew the clip in place (see **Fig F**).

F

NECKLACE

1 For the necklace, double thread a beading needle with embroidery thread. Make a couple of tiny stitches at the base of the doll's neck at the back to secure the thread in position, then thread seed beads onto this.

2 Stitch the other end of the necklace in the same spot at the back of the neck to ensure the necklace stays in place.

PATTERNS
Little Mermaid

Also use the Head and Arm patterns from the Basic Doll project (see How to Sew the Basic Doll).
All the patterns are actual size, so there is no need to reduce or enlarge them.

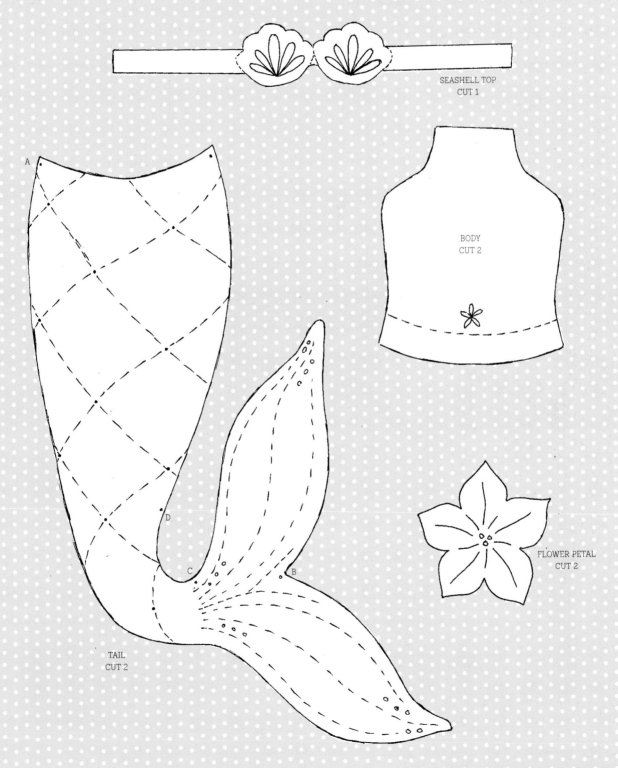

SEASHELL TOP
CUT 1

BODY
CUT 2

FLOWER PETAL
CUT 2

TAIL
CUT 2

GIRLS' Night Out

DRESSING UP IS REALLY FUN, ESPECIALLY IF YOU'RE GOING SOMEWHERE SPECIAL! THIS ELEGANTLY DRESSED GIRL IS HEADING OFF TO THE THEATRE TO WATCH HER BEST FRIEND PERFORM WITH THE ROYAL BALLET COMPANY. SHE WEARS A FORM-FITTING SCALLOP SLEEVE DRESS EDGED IN BLACK LACE, AND HER DARLING LITTLE SHOES ARE TIED ABOUT HER ANKLES WITH RIBBON. A SMART CLUTCH AND WIDE BELT COMPLETE THE LOOK.

YOU WILL Need

- MATERIALS FOR THE BASIC DOLL PROJECT (SEE HOW TO SEW THE BASIC DOLL)
- LACE TRIM FOR DRESS HEM, 11.5CM (4½IN) LENGTH
- RIBBON FOR THE BELT, 11.5CM (4½IN) LENGTH, 1CM (⅜IN) WIDTH
- RIBBON FOR THE SANDALS, 25CM (10IN) LENGTH, 3MM (⅛IN) WIDTH
- SMALL SQUARE SEQUIN FOR THE CLUTCH • SNAP CLOSURE FOR THE BELT, 5MM (³⁄₁₆) DIAMETER
- FRAY CHECK LIQUID • 5 X 7.5CM (2 X 3IN) CARDSTOCK FOR THE INNER SOLES OF THE SANDALS

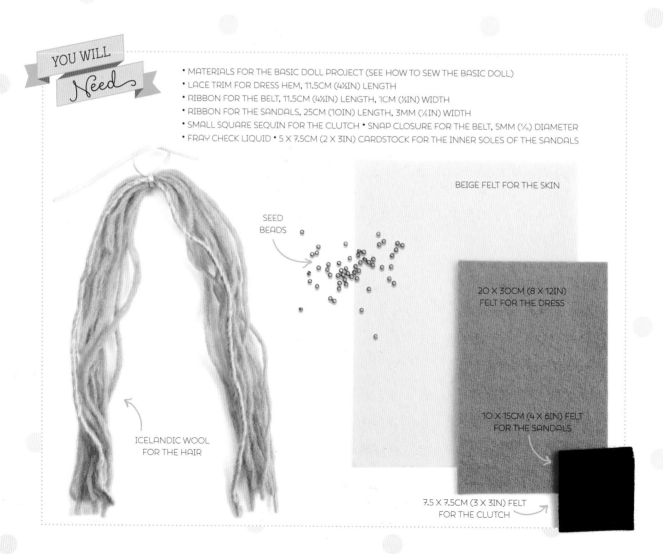

SEED BEADS

BEIGE FELT FOR THE SKIN

20 X 30CM (8 X 12IN) FELT FOR THE DRESS

10 X 15CM (4 X 6IN) FELT FOR THE SANDALS

ICELANDIC WOOL FOR THE HAIR

7.5 X 7.5CM (3 X 3IN) FELT FOR THE CLUTCH

CUTTING AND ASSEMBLY

1 Follow the steps for making the Basic Doll up to Step 10 of the Hair section (see How to Sew the Basic Doll).

DRESS

1 Using your disappearing ink marker, transfer the markings shown on the dress pattern to the pieces of felt you have cut for it.

2 Fold the dress in half at the shoulders, wrong sides facing, then pin. Whip stitch (see Stitch Guide) the side seams together, starting at the dot below each armhole and working down to the hem (see **Fig A**).

3 Using black embroidery thread (floss), blanket stitch (see Stitch Guide) around the neckline of the dress, starting at the asterisk at the back of the dress and working up the side of the back, around the neckline and down to the asterisk at the opposite side. Then sew seed beads onto the dots marked around the front neckline (see **Fig A**).

4 From the wrong side of the felt, pin lace trim along the bottom edge of the dress hem then sew in place with tiny stitches (see **Fig A**).

5 Whip stitch the back edges of the dress together, again starting at the asterisk, but this time working down to the hem (see **Fig A**).

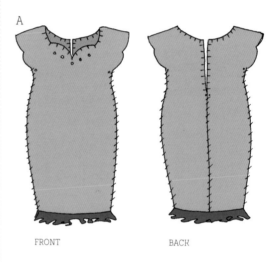

A

FRONT   BACK

6 For the belt, apply a small bead of Fray Check to each cut end of the 1cm (½in) wide ribbon then allow to dry thoroughly.

7 Wrap the ribbon around the doll's waist, so the cut ends are at the back of doll. Determine where to position the snap closure on the belt, mark each spot with your disappearing ink marker, then remove the belt and sew the discs in place.

CLUTCH

1 Using your disappearing ink marker, first transfer the dotted lines and marks indicated on the pattern of the clutch onto the piece of felt you have cut for it.

2 Fold the bottom section A of the clutch at the dotted line, aligning its side edges with those of section B, and pin. Whip stitch the sides of sections A and B together, leaving the top edge open, then add a little stuffing inside to fill it out a bit (see **Fig B**).

FRONT

3 Now turn the clutch over so the back of the bag is facing up towards you. Centre the square sequin where the two scalloped edges meet at the top edge of the clutch, then sew in place, adding a seed bead in the middle (see **Fig C**). Do not end off your thread yet.

4 Fold section C onto section A, then pin in place. Using a couple of tiny stitches, stitch the front flap down onto the front of the bag, taking the stitches through to the back of the bag (see **Fig C**).

BACK

SHOES

1 Using your disappearing ink marker, transfer the markings shown on the shoe pattern to the pieces of felt you have cut for them.

2 To make one shoe, take two of the felt soles and one cardstock sole. Squeeze a little blob of glue onto a piece of scrap paper then use a cotton bud (Q-tip) to apply a thin layer of glue to one side of the cardstock.

3 Position the cardstock sole onto the bottom felt sole, using the dots marked on the heels and at the toe to check the alignment. You'll find that the inner cardstock sole is slightly smaller than the felt sole to allow the top and bottom felt soles to be stitched together later on.

4 Apply a thin layer of glue to the top of the cardstock sole and stick the top felt sole onto the top of the pile, making sure everything is centred and the dots are aligned (see **Fig D**).

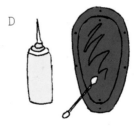

D

5 Now repeat Steps 1 to 4 for the second shoe and allow the glue on both to dry.

6 Blanket stitch the edge between the dots marked B on each shoe top. Sew three seed beads onto the left-hand side of one top and three onto the right-hand side of the other, using the marked dots as a guide (see **Fig E**).

7 Position one shoe top onto a sole, aligning dot A at the centre of the shoe top with the dot at the centre of sole, then pin in place. Working from dot A around to dot B on each side, blanket stitch the shoe top onto the sole (see **Fig E**).

E

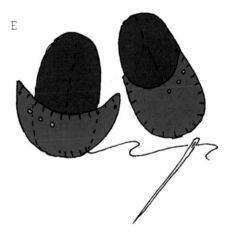

8 Fold the two tabs you have cut for the heels at the centre, so dots C match. Then blanket stitch the bottom edges of the tabs together (see **Fig F**).

F

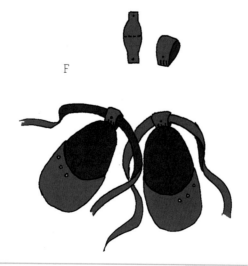

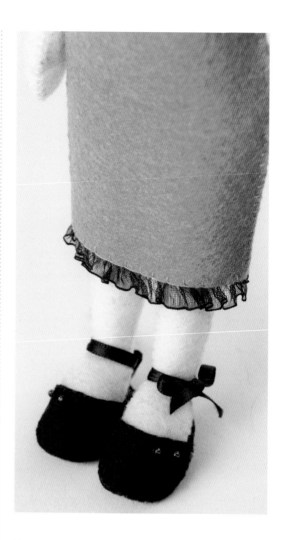

9 Pin the stitched edges of each tab to the heels of the soles, aligning the dots at C. Then blanket stitch the edge of each tab onto the edge of the sole (see **Fig F**).

10 Cut the 3mm (⅛in) wide ribbon in half. Insert one length of ribbon through the little loop of the heel tab then fit the shoe onto the doll, tying the ribbon around the ankle. Repeat for the other shoe to complete (see **Fig F**).

PATTERNS
Girls' Night Out

Also use the patterns from the Basic Doll project
(see How to Sew the Basic Doll).
All the patterns are actual size, so there is
no need to enlarge or reduce them.

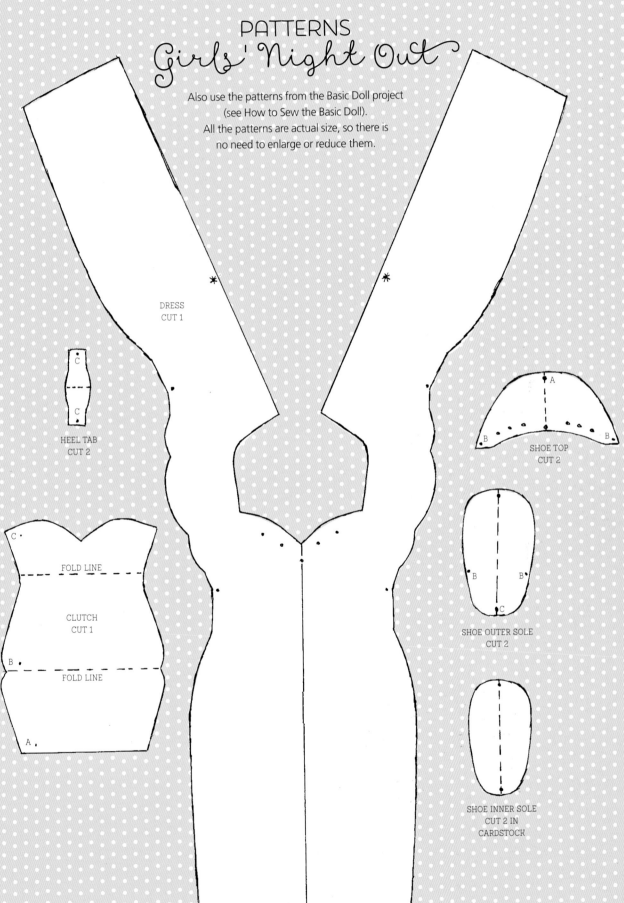

DRESS
CUT 1

HEEL TAB
CUT 2

SHOE TOP
CUT 2

CLUTCH
CUT 1

FOLD LINE

FOLD LINE

SHOE OUTER SOLE
CUT 2

SHOE INNER SOLE
CUT 2 IN
CARDSTOCK

FLOWER
Fairy

IF YOU'VE EVER WANDERED DOWN THE GARDEN PATH EARLY ON A SPRING MORNING,
YOU MAY HAVE CAUGHT A GLIMPSE OF SHIMMERY GOSSAMER WINGS AND HEARD
THE SOUND OF TINY TINKLING BELLS – NOW IT'S TIME TO MAKE YOUR VERY OWN
FLOWER FAIRY! THIS SHY GARDEN FAIRY WEARS A SIMPLE HALTER-NECK SUNDRESS
SPRINKLED WITH FLOWER SEQUINS AND SHINY BEADS. HER DELICATE WINGS, WHICH
ARE EASILY REMOVABLE, SPARKLE WITH TINY SWAROVSKI CRYSTALS, AND HER
HEADBAND AND SLIPPERS ARE ACCENTED WITH BEADED FLOWER BLOSSOMS.

YOU WILL Need

- MATERIALS FOR THE BASIC DOLL PROJECT (SEE HOW TO SEW THE BASIC DOLL)
- MATCHING EMBROIDERY THREAD (FLOSS) • RIBBON FOR THE HEADBAND, 30CM (12IN) LENGTH,
5MM (¼IN) WIDTH • SNAP CLOSURE FOR THE DRESS, 5MM (¼IN) DIAMETER
- SNAP CLOSURE FOR ATTACHING THE WINGS, 9MM (⅜IN) DIAMETER
- ,WAROVSKI CRYSTALS • FRAY CHECK LIQUID • TWEEZERS

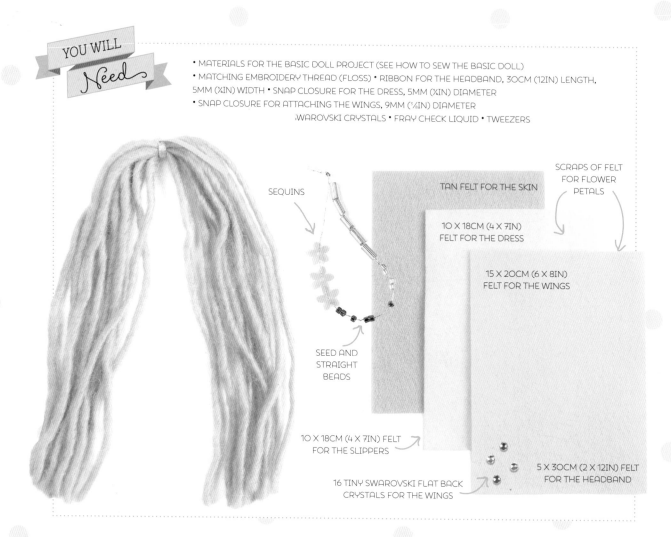

SEQUINS

SEED AND STRAIGHT BEADS

TAN FELT FOR THE SKIN

10 X 18CM (4 X 7IN)
FELT FOR THE DRESS

SCRAPS OF FELT
FOR FLOWER
PETALS

15 X 20CM (6 X 8IN)
FELT FOR THE WINGS

10 X 18CM (4 X 7IN) FELT
FOR THE SLIPPERS

16 TINY SWAROVSKI FLAT BACK
CRYSTALS FOR THE WINGS

5 X 30CM (2 X 12IN) FELT
FOR THE HEADBAND

CUTTING AND ASSEMBLY

1 Follow the steps for making the Basic Doll up to Step 9 of the Hair section (see How to Sew the Basic Doll).

HAIR

1 To style the doll's hair, lift the top loose layer of strands up and away from the glued bottom layer, and make sure all the strands on the bottom layer are even and straight across.

2 Starting at the centre of the neck and working out towards each side, carefully cut the strands so that they just touch the shoulders. Take your time to check that each side is even and don't pull the strands too tightly, as they will spring up a bit once settled.

3 When the bottom layer is cut, arrange the top layer of strands over the bottom layer, making sure they are even and straight. Using the bottom layer as a guide, cut the top strands to evenly match the bottom edge.

4 For the fringe, cut three or four strands of wool (yarn) so that they're just touching the eyes, making sure you don't tug on them as you cut. Also cut a few graduated strands on either side of the face to achieve a soft layered look.

DRESS

1 Using your disappearing ink marker, transfer all the markings shown on the dress front and back patterns to the pieces of felt you have cut for them. Then sew sequins and beads onto the dots around the front neckline, and the front and back hems (see **Fig A**).

A

2 Line up the front hem of the dress with the back hem and pin at the sides. Then whip stitch (see Stitch Guide) the sides of the dress together, beginning at the asterisk below each armhole and working down to end at the asterisk just above the hem of the dress.

3 Now blanket stitch (see Stitch Guide) around the entire outer edge of the dress, starting at the base of the armhole and working around the outer and inner straps of the neckline, around the opposite armhole then around the back edge of the dress. This will reinforce these openings and prevent them from warping while you dress the doll.

4 To finish the dress, fit it onto the doll to determine the position for the snap closure on the neck strap. Remove the dress and sew the 5mm (¼in) snap closure onto the back of the neck opening. Then sew the female side of the 9mm (⅜in) snap closure for the wings onto the back of the dress onto the X marking (see **Fig B**).

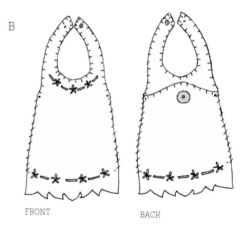

B

FRONT   BACK

FAIRY WINGS

1 Using your disappearing ink marker, transfer all the markings shown on the wing patterns to the pieces of felt you have cut for them. Then sew the male side of the 9mm (⅜in) snap closure onto the front facing wing (see **Fig C**).

2 Now place the front facing wing onto the back wing, making sure that all the edges are aligned, then blanket stitch around the entire edge of the wings (see **Fig C**). Double-siding them like this will help prevent them from drooping.

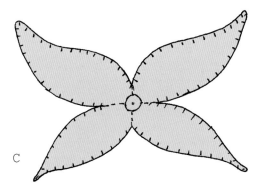

C

3 Squeeze a little blob of glue onto a piece of scrap paper. Use your tweezers to carefully pick up a Swarovski crystal, making sure that the flat back is facing down. Gently dip the back of the crystal into the glue, then place it onto one of the dot markings at the tips of the wings. Continue working in this manner until all the crystals have been glued in place, then allow to dry thoroughly (see **Fig D**).

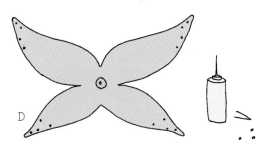

D

FLOWER SLIPPERS

1 Using your disappearing ink marker, first transfer the dots, the X marking and the ruled lines shown on the slipper front and sole patterns onto the felt pieces you have cut for them. Also transfer the markings onto the two small flower petals A.

2 Using one strand of embroidery thread (floss) and with one small flower, embroider the centre line of each petal. Then stitch three seed beads onto the centre of the flower (see **Fig E**).

E

3 Blanket stitch around the inner edge of the slipper top (see **Fig F**).

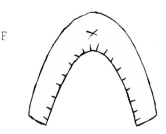

F

4 Position the flower onto the X marking on the slipper front, then sew in place using a few tiny stitches at the flower centre (see **Fig G**).

G

5 Now fold the slipper top in half and whip stitch the back ends together (see **Fig H**).

6 Place the felt piece you cut for the sole onto the bottom of the slipper top, aligning the dots at the heel and toe, then blanket stitch the sole onto the slipper top (see **Fig I**).

H   I

7 Repeat Steps 1 to 6 to complete the other slipper.

FLOWER HEADBAND

1 Using your disappearing ink marker, first transfer the two dots on either end of the headband pattern onto the back of the piece of felt you have cut for it. Also ensure you have transferred all the dots shown on the headband pattern onto the front of the felt headband; the dots marked A will correspond to the smaller flowers A, and the dots marked B will correspond to the larger flowers B.

2 With one strand of embroidery thread, embroider the centre line of each petal for each of the six flowers. Stitch three seed beads onto the centre of each flower, keeping a length of thread at the back of each so you can sew the flower onto the headband later (see **Fig J**).

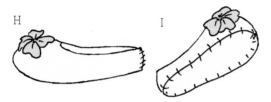

J

3 Blanket stitch around the entire edge of the headband.

4 Now cut two pieces of your ribbon, each measuring 15cm (6in) in length. Apply a small bead of Fray Check liquid to either end of the cut ribbon lengths and allow this to dry thoroughly.

5 Position one end of a ribbon length onto the dot marked at the back of the felt headband and use straight stitches to sew this in place, keeping your stitches small and neat, then repeat this process at the other end for the second piece. These pieces of ribbon will be used to tie the flower headband at the back of the doll's head (see **Fig K**).

K

BACK

6 Position each flower onto the corresponding dot on the front of the headband. Using the thread at the back of each flower, stitch each flower centre in place (see **Fig L**), then fit the headband onto your doll.

L

PATTERNS
Flower Fairy

Also use the patterns from the Basic Doll project (see How to Sew the Basic Doll). All the patterns are shown at actual size, so there is no need to enlarge or reduce them.

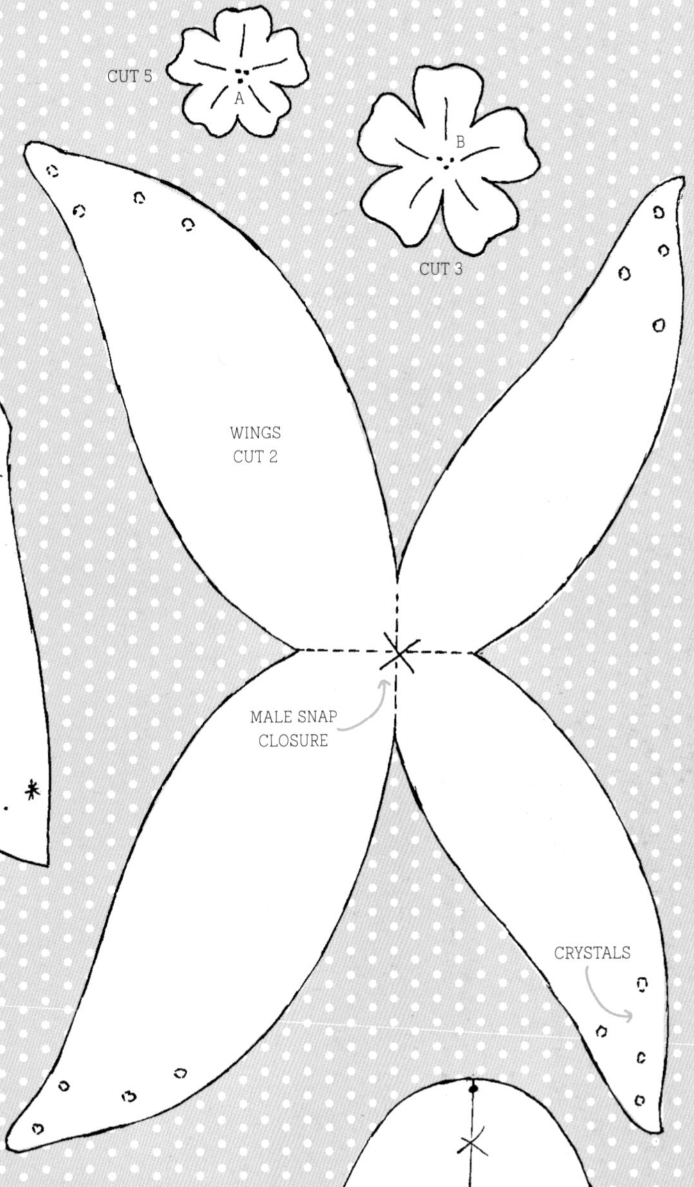

HEADBAND CUT 1

CUT 5

A

B

CUT 3

DRESS FRONT
CUT 1

WINGS
CUT 2

MALE SNAP
CLOSURE

CRYSTALS

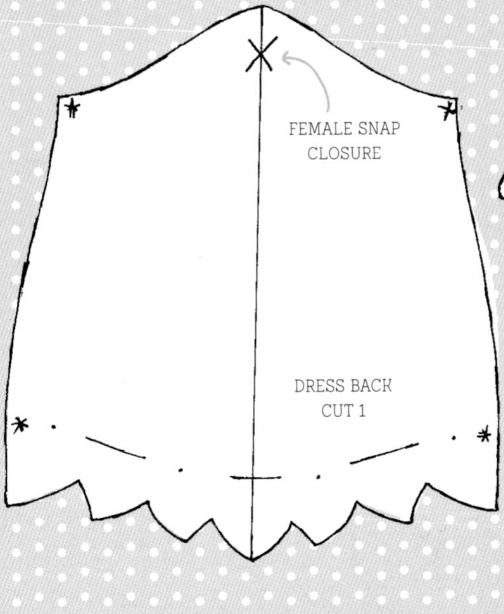

FEMALE SNAP
CLOSURE

DRESS BACK
CUT 1

SLIPPER SOLE
CUT 2

SLIPPER TOP
CUT 2

BEACH
Babe

IT'S A PERFECT DAY TO HEAD TO THE BEACH! THIS SWEET, SUN-KISSED
BEACH BABE IS READY FOR THE SURF, WEARING HER PRETTY PINK
POLKA-DOT BIKINI, MATCHING SANDALS AND A BIG FLOPPY HAT TO
SHADE HER EYES FROM THE SUN. AND DON'T FORGET TO BRING ALONG
THE BEACH BAG TO HOLD HER TOWEL, BOOK AND SUNSCREEN!

YOU WILL *Need*

- MATERIALS FOR THE BASIC DOLL PROJECT (SEE HOW TO SEW THE BASIC DOLL)
- SMALL BUTTON PIN OR COILESS SAFETY PIN • TWO SNAP CLOSURES, 5MM (³⁄₁₆IN) DIAMETER
- 5 X 15CM (2 X 6IN) CARDSTOCK FOR THE INNER SOLES OF THE SANDALS

15 X 20CM (6 X 8IN) FELT
FOR THE BEACH BAG

TAN FELT FOR
THE SKIN

5 X 15CM (2 X 6IN) FELT
FOR THE SANDAL SOLES

10 X 15CM (4 X 6IN)
FELT FOR THE BIKINI
AND SANDAL STRAPS

4.5 X 25CM (1¾ X 10IN) FELT
FOR THE DECORATIVE BAND

ICELANDIC WOOL
FOR THE HAIR

TWO PIECES OF 20 X 30CM (8 X 12IN)
FELT FOR THE FLOPPY HAT

10 X 15CM (4 X 6IN)
FELT FOR THE BOWS

CUTTING AND ASSEMBLY

1 Follow steps for making the Basic Doll up to Step 10 of the Hair section (see How to Sew the Basic Doll).

BIKINI TOP

1 Using your disappearing ink marker, transfer the X markings shown on the bikini top and bow patterns to the pieces of felt you have cut for them.

2 Using a strand of embroidery thread (floss), blanket stitch (see Stitch Guide) all around the edges of the bikini top (see **Fig A**). This will reinforce the edges and prevent them from warping when you are dressing the doll.

A

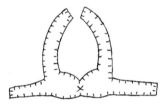

3 On the smaller felt bow A, embroider the X detail at the centre, following the markings you transferred with your disappearing ink pen.

4 Position the smaller felt bow on top of the larger one B, aligning the centre of the top bow in the centre of the larger bow. Then carefully place the double bow stack onto the centre of the bikini top and using tiny vertical stitches, stitch them in place with embroidery thread (see **Fig B**).

B

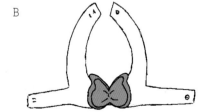

5 Fit the bikini top onto the doll, mark the position for the snap closures then sew each of these in place.

BIKINI BOTTOMS

1 Using your disappearing ink marker, transfer the two X markings shown on the bikini bottoms pattern to the piece of felt you have cut for them.

2 Fold the bikini bottoms in half at the crotch, wrong sides facing, then whip stitch (see Stitch Guide) the sides together.

3 Blanket stitch around the waistband and leg openings (see **Fig C**). This will reinforce the edges and prevent them from warping while you are dressing the doll.

4 Stitch the centre of each bow C onto the X you marked on either side of the of the front section (see **Fig D**).

C   D

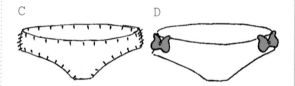

BEACH BAG

1 Using your disappearing ink marker, transfer the X markings shown on the beach bag pattern to the piece of felt you have cut for it.

2 Blanket stitch one long edge of the bag bottom to the bottom edge of the front piece of the beach bag, then repeat this with the back piece (see **Fig E**).

3 Now blanket stitch the short edge of one bag side onto a short side of the bag bottom, then repeat by stitching the second bag side onto the opposite side of the bag bottom (see **Fig E**).

E

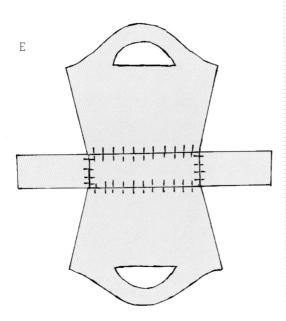

4 Blanket stitch the long edges of both bag sides to the sides of the front and back of the bag. Then blanket stitch all around the top edge of the bag, as well as inside the handle.

5 On the smaller felt bow D, follow the markings you transferred with your disappearing ink pen to embroider the X detail at the centre of the bow.

6 Place the smaller felt bow onto the larger felt bow E, positioning the centre of the top bow in the centre of the larger one. Carefully place the bow stack onto the X marked at the base of the handle then sew the centre of the bow onto the bag (see **Fig F**).

F

FLOPPY HAT

1 Using your disappearing ink marker, transfer the X marking shown on the smaller hat bow pattern F to the piece of felt you have cut for it.

2 Whip stitch the short sides of the hatband together. Pin the crown on top, then blanket stitch all the way around to fix this to the hatband (see **Fig G**).

3 Position the open bottom edge of the hatband onto the inner opening of the hat brim, then whip stitch them together (see **Fig G**).

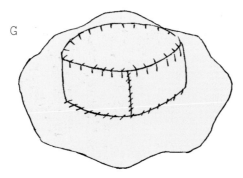

G

4 Now pin the decorative band to the hatband, aligning the short sides with the hatband's seam; the bottom long edge of the decorative band should be perfectly aligned with the whip-stitched seam where the brim joins the band. Whip stitch the short sides of the band together, then use tiny stitches to fix the band in place just inside each long edge (see **Fig H**).

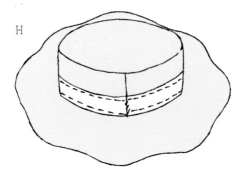

H

5 On the smaller felt bow F, use straight stitches to embroider the X detail at its centre, following the markings you transferred earlier.

6 Place the smaller felt bow onto the larger felt bow G, aligning their centres, then stitch it in place with embroidery thread.

7 Insert a button pin into the back of the bow. Fit the hat on the doll then fold a small section of the brim up towards the hatband and position the bow onto the folded area, pinning it in place (see **Fig I**).

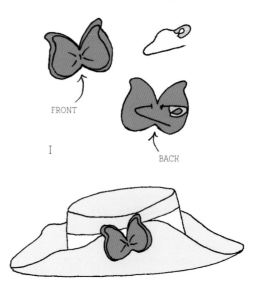

FRONT

I

BACK

SANDALS

1 Follow steps 1 to 5 of the Shoes section from the Girls' Night Out project (see Girls' Night Out).

2 Now blanket stitch around the sole of each sandal (see **Fig J**).

3 Continuing to work on the first sandal, ensure you have clearly transferred the dot markings A, B, C and D, and the X, from the sandal strap pattern piece onto the felt sandal top. Then blanket stitch around the top and bottom edge of the sandal strap, but do not blanket stitch the short sides yet (see **Fig K**).

4 Embroider the X detail at the centre of bow H, following the markings you transferred with your disappearing ink pen.

5 Position the bow onto the strap and stitch the centre of the bow onto the X marked at the centre.

6 Align the short edges of the sandal strap with the dots marked on the sole, matching the corresponding letters A and B on the left. Then blanket stitch the sides of the sandal strap to the sole. Repeat on the right side of the sandal with dots C and D.

7 Repeat Steps 2 to 6 to complete the other sandal (see **Fig L**).

Tip

ALTERNATIVELY, YOU COULD OMIT THE FELT BOW FROM THE SANDAL STRAP FOR A SIMPLER LOOK, OR EMBELLISH THE STRAP WITH SEQUINS AND SEED BEADS.

PATTERNS
Beach Babe

Also use the patterns from the Basic Doll project (see How to Sew the Basic Doll).
All the patterns are actual size, so there is no need to enlarge or reduce them.

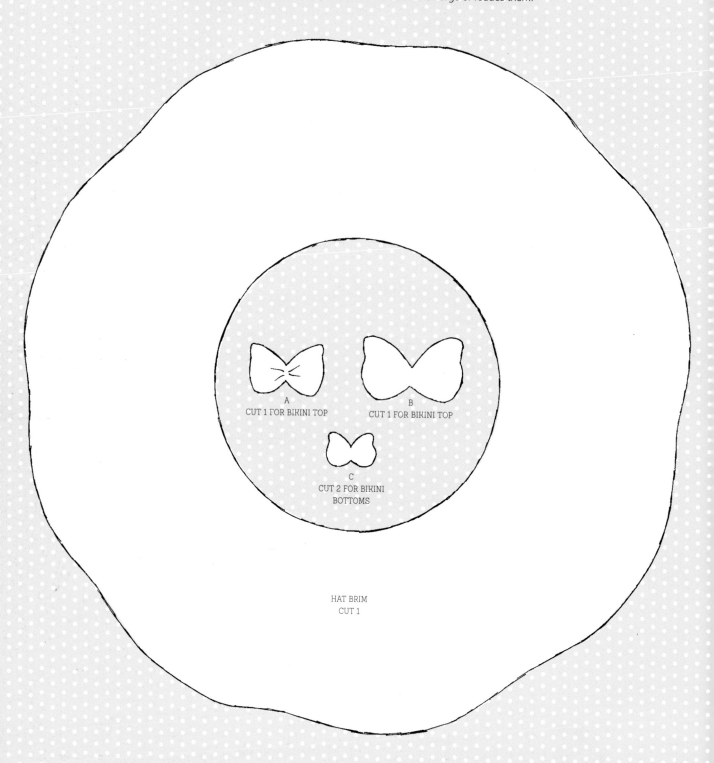

A
CUT 1 FOR BIKINI TOP

B
CUT 1 FOR BIKINI TOP

C
CUT 2 FOR BIKINI
BOTTOMS

HAT BRIM
CUT 1

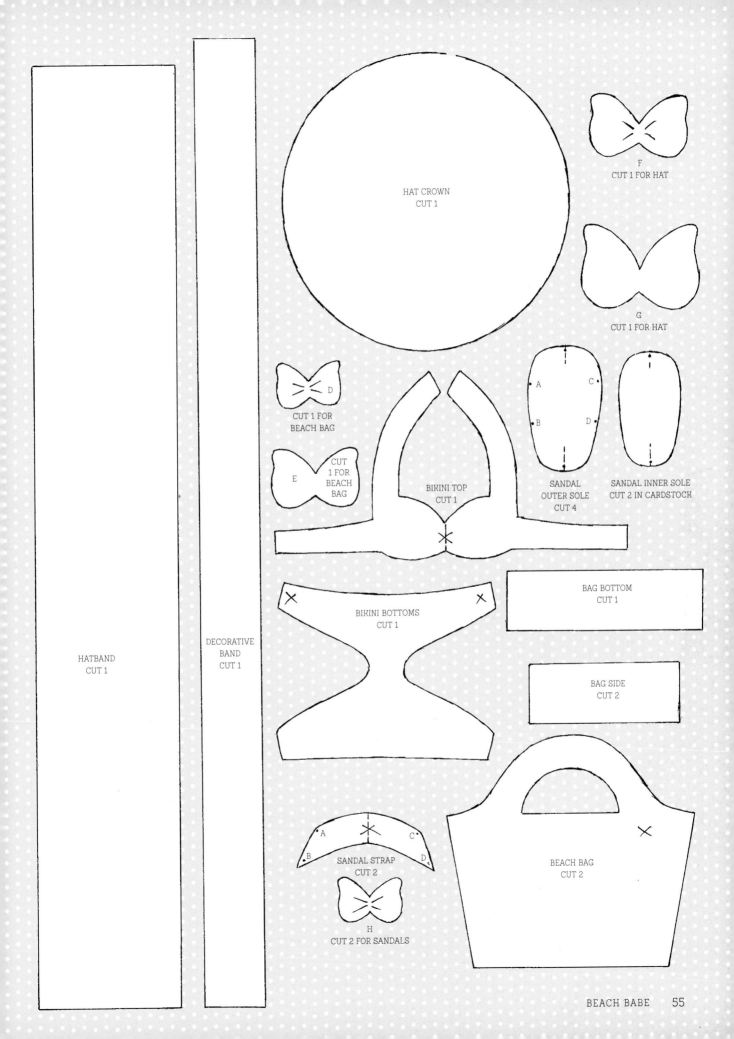

HATBAND
CUT 1

DECORATIVE
BAND
CUT 1

HAT CROWN
CUT 1

F
CUT 1 FOR HAT

G
CUT 1 FOR HAT

D
CUT 1 FOR
BEACH BAG

E
CUT
1 FOR
BEACH
BAG

BIKINI TOP
CUT 1

A
C
B
D
SANDAL
OUTER SOLE
CUT 4

SANDAL INNER SOLE
CUT 2 IN CARDSTOCK

BIKINI BOTTOMS
CUT 1

BAG BOTTOM
CUT 1

BAG SIDE
CUT 2

A
C
B
D
SANDAL STRAP
CUT 2

H
CUT 2 FOR SANDALS

BEACH BAG
CUT 2

PRIMA Ballerina

THIS BUDDING LITTLE PRIMA BALLERINA IS DRESSED IN A PRETTY PINK LEOTARD ADORNED WITH DAZZLING SEQUINS AND SEED BEADS THAT SPARKLE AT THE NECKLINE. HER TUTU IS FULL AND FLUFFY, AND MADE FROM DOZENS OF TULLE STRIPS LOOPED AROUND A SIMPLE RIBBON WAISTBAND. DELICATE RIBBONS ON HER BALLET SLIPPERS ARE CRISSCROSSED AROUND HER LEGS AND TIED JUST BEHIND HER KNEES. FINALLY, A LITTLE FLORAL HAIR CLIP IS CLIPPED INTO THE BALLERINA'S HAIR TO ACCENTUATE THE PRETTY LITTLE BUN AT THE BACK OF HER HEAD.

YOU WILL Need

- MATERIALS FOR THE BASIC DOLL PROJECT (SEE HOW TO SEW THE BASIC DOLL)
- SMALL HOOK AND EYE CLOSURE • TINY METAL HAIR CLIP, 2CM (¾IN) LENGTH
- FOUR OR FIVE SMALL HAIR CLAMPS WITH TEETH

SCRAPS OF FELT FOR THE FLORAL HAIR ACCESSORY

RIBBON FOR THE SHOELACES, 1M (40IN) LENGTH, 5MM (¼IN) WIDTH

ICELANDIC WOOL FOR THE HAIR

RIBBON FOR THE TUTU'S WAISTBAND, 38CM (15IN) LENGTH, 1CM (⅜IN) WIDTH

BLUSH FELT FOR THE SKIN

10 X 18CM (4 X 7IN) FELT FOR THE BALLET SLIPPERS

SEQUINS

10 X 18CM (4 X 7IN) FELT FOR THE LEOTARD

SEED BEADS

127 X 15CM (50 X 6IN) TULLE FOR THE TUTU

CUTTING AND ASSEMBLY

1 Follow the steps for making the Basic Doll up to Step 10 of the Hair section (see How to Sew the Basic Doll).

HAIR

1 To make the little bun, first gather the hair at the base of the neck, smoothing all the strands together, and gently twist all the way down its length.

2 Coil the twisted strands at the back of the head to form the bun, tucking any edges of the hair that protrude underneath it. Now pin hair clamps around the base of bun to keep it in place.

3 Thread a long needle with double embroidery thread (floss) to match the hair colour and sew the bun onto the hair. Then carefully remove the hair clamps.

LEOTARD

1 Using your disappearing ink marker, transfer the dot markings shown on the leotard pattern front to the front piece of leotard felt. Then sew sequins and seed beads onto each dot around the neckline.

2 Line up the front of the leotard with the leotard back and pin at the shoulders. Then blanket stitch (see Stitch Guide) these shoulder seams together (see **Fig A**).

3 Whip stitch (see Stitch Guide) the sides of the leotard together, beginning at the dot marked below each armhole and ending at the leg opening (see **Fig A**).

4 Blanket stitch around the entire edge of the neckline, as well as each armhole and both leg openings. This will reinforce these openings and prevent them from warping when you are dressing the doll (see **Fig A**).

A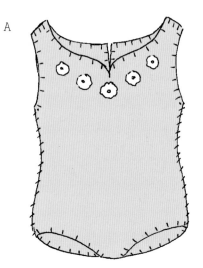

5 To finish the leotard, sew the hook and eye closure onto the back of the neck opening then fit the leotard onto the doll, in preparation for making the tutu. You will find that the leotard may push up the doll's arms a bit into a pretty pose, as was the case with my doll.

TUTU

1 With the leotard already fitted, tie your length of 1cm (½in) width ribbon around the doll's waist, making a bow at the back of her body. With your disappearing ink marker, add a dot to your ribbon at each side of the bow, as guides for attaching the tulle in the next step.

2 Beginning at one dot, start to loop and tie your tulle strips around the ribbon as shown. Repeat this process until you fill the ribbon and reach the dot at the opposite end (see **Fig B**).

3 Fit the tutu onto the doll, adding more strips if needed to make the effect nice and fluffy. Then trim the edge of the tulle to even out the bottom (see **Fig C**)

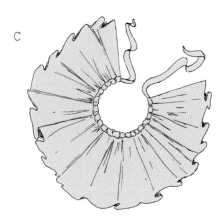

C

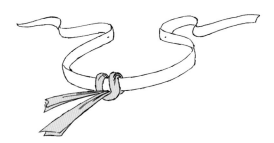

B

BALLET SLIPPERS

1 Using your disappearing ink marker, first transfer the dots shown on the slipper front and sole patterns onto the felt slipper fronts and soles you have cut.

2 To make one slipper, first stitch a sequin and seed bead onto the inside dot and blanket stitch around the inner edge of the slipper top (see **Fig D**).

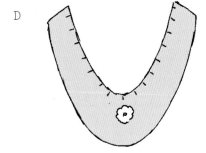

D

3 Now fold the slipper top in half and whip stitch the back ends together (see **Fig E**).

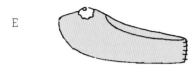

E

4 Place the felt sole piece onto the bottom of the slipper top, aligning the dots on both pieces at the heel and toe. Then blanket stitch the sole onto the slipper top (see **Fig F**).

F

5 Each slipper will require two ribbons. To make a pair, first cut your length of 5mm (¼in) ribbon into four pieces so each measures 25cm (10in) in length. Tuck one ribbon edge into the back of the slipper on one side of the back seam and sew this in place, then repeat this process with the other edge (see **Fig G**).

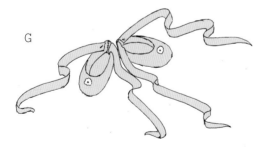

G

6 Place the finished slipper on your doll and wrap the ribbons around her leg, making a pretty bow at the back of the leg.

7 Repeat Steps 1 to 6 to make the other slipper.

FLOWER PETAL HAIR ACCESSORY

1 Stitch the bottom end of the leaf onto the petal base (see **Fig H**).

H

2 Position one flower petal on top of the base so that it overlaps the area of the leaf that has already been sewn down. Stitch the centre of the petal in place using one or two tiny stitches. Then stitch a seed bead onto the centre of the flower petal.

3 Take the thread through to the back of the flower base. Position the second flower onto the flower base, slightly overlapping the first leaf and petal, then stitch into place using one or two tiny stitches. Stitch a seed bead onto the centre of the second petal (see **Fig I**).

I

4 Position the hair clip onto the petal base and sew the clip in place then add to your doll (see **Fig J**).

J

PATTERNS
Prima Ballerina

Also use the patterns from the Basic Doll project (see How to Sew the Basic Doll).
All the patterns are actual size, so there is no need to enlarge or reduce them.

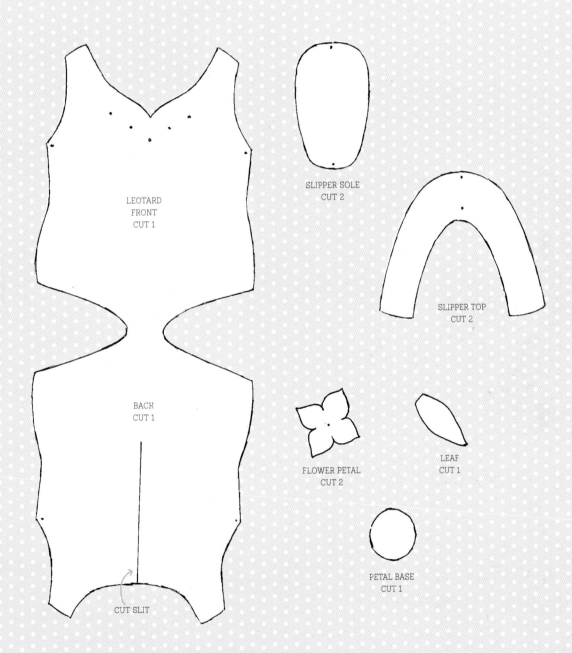

LEOTARD
FRONT
CUT 1

SLIPPER SOLE
CUT 2

SLIPPER TOP
CUT 2

BACK
CUT 1

FLOWER PETAL
CUT 2

LEAF
CUT 1

PETAL BASE
CUT 1

CUT SLIT

LITTLE
Princess

WHO DOESN'T LOVE PRETENDING TO BE A PRINCESS FOR A DAY? IT'S THE
MOST WONDERFUL FEELING IN THE WORLD! AND A GLITTERY TIARA AND
SPARKLING SLIPPERS ARE ALL PART OF THE FUN. THIS HAPPY GIRL IS
PRACTISING HER TWIRLS AND CURTSEYS, AND LOOKS SIMPLY ADORABLE
IN HER DELICATELY EMBROIDERED AND BEADED BLOUSE AND SKIRT.

YOU WILL *Need*

- MATERIALS FOR THE BASIC DOLL PROJECT (SEE HOW TO SEW THE BASIC DOLL)
- METALLIC AND REGULAR EMBROIDERY THREAD (FLOSS) • SEED BEADS • GLITTER
- TWO SNAP CLOSURES FOR THE BLOUSE, 5MM (¼IN) DIAMETER • CLEAR DRYING CRAFT GLUE
- SMALL HOOK AND EYE CLOSURE FOR THE SKIRT • PENCIL
- CARDBOARD ROLL FROM AN EMPTY PAPER TOWEL OR TOILET PAPER HOLDER

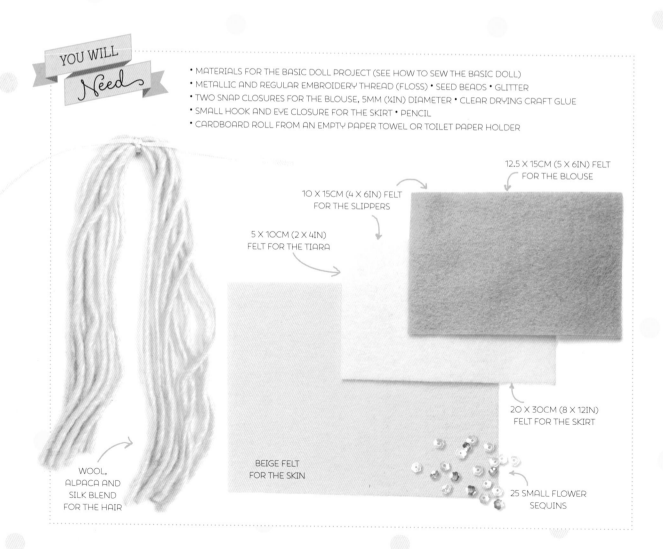

12.5 X 15CM (5 X 6IN) FELT
FOR THE BLOUSE

10 X 15CM (4 X 6IN) FELT
FOR THE SLIPPERS

5 X 10CM (2 X 4IN)
FELT FOR THE TIARA

20 X 30CM (8 X 12IN)
FELT FOR THE SKIRT

BEIGE FELT
FOR THE SKIN

WOOL,
ALPACA AND
SILK BLEND
FOR THE HAIR

25 SMALL FLOWER
SEQUINS

LAYOUT AND CUTTING

1 Follow the steps for making the Basic Doll up to Step 4 of the Layout and Cutting section (see How to Sew the Basic Doll), using the face pattern provided for this project instead of the Basic Doll.

HEAD

1 With your disappearing ink marker, transfer the facial markings shown on the face pattern onto the piece of felt you have cut for it.

2 Using one strand of embroidery thread (floss), outline the eyes with stem stitch (see Stitch Guide). Then make a couple of tiny straight stitches, very close together, just below the eye for the beauty spot.

3 Outline the central line of the mouth then the upper and lower lip in stem stitch. Fill in the top lip with satin stitch (see Stitch Guide) and follow with the lower lip.

4 Now follow Steps 5 to 6 of the Head section from the Basic Doll project (see How to Sew the Basic Doll) omitting to embroider the eyelashes.

ASSEMBLING THE BASIC DOLL

1 Follow the steps for making the Basic Doll from Step 1 of the Assembling the Head section up to Step 10 of the Hair section (see How to Sew the Basic Doll).

BLOUSE

1 With your disappearing ink marker, first transfer all the dots and markings shown on the blouse pattern onto the felt pieces you have cut for it.

2 Using metallic embroidery thread and stem stitch (see Stitch Guide), embroider a vertical line between each of the top and bottom dots shown on the blouse pattern then sew a seed bead onto each dot (see **Fig A**).

3 Fold the blouse in half at the shoulders, wrong sides facing, then pin. Whip stitch (see Stitch Guide) the side seams together, starting at the dot below each armhole and working down to the hem (see **Fig A**).

4 Now blanket stitch (see Stitch Guide) around the back edges, neckline, hem and armholes of the blouse (see **Fig A**). This will reinforce these openings and prevent them from warping while you are dressing the doll.

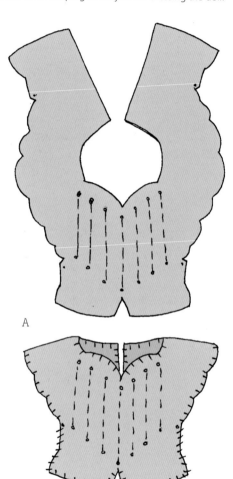

A

5 Fit the blouse onto the doll with the opening down the back. Determine where to fix the two snap closures, then remove the blouse from the doll and sew them in place.

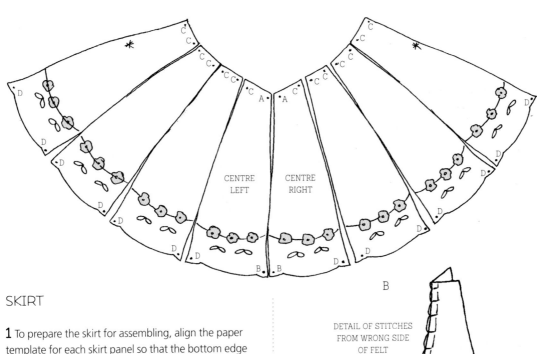

CENTRE LEFT

CENTRE RIGHT

SKIRT

1 To prepare the skirt for assembling, align the paper template for each skirt panel so that the bottom edge of each template matches the bottom edge of the skirt panel and the dots marked E align with each other. Using your disappearing ink marker, transfer the vertical central line onto each skirt panel, as well as the curved horizontal line at the top of the hem, and the dot and leaf markings.

2 Using metallic embroidery thread, embroider the curved horizontal line on each skirt panel in stem stitch. Then sew a sequin with a seed bead at the centre of each dot above the hem, and use lazy daisy stitch (see Stitch Guide) to sew the leaf designs below the sequins (see **Fig B**).

3 Position the centre left and right front panels together, right sides facing, so dots A are matching at the waistband and dots B match at the hem. Pin in place, then blanket stitch the edges together from A to B. Now back stitch (see Stitch Guide) just below the blanket stitches from A to B, positioning the stitches between each blanket stitch (see **Fig B**) to help create a nice crisp edge.

B

DETAIL OF STITCHES
FROM WRONG SIDE
OF FELT

4 Position a side panel onto the centre right panel, right sides facing, so dots C are matching at the waistband and dots D match at the hem. Pin in place, then blanket stitch the edge from C to D. Now back stitch just below the blanket stitches from C to D, positioning the stitches between each blanket stitch (see **Fig B**).

5 Repeat Step 4 on the opposite side, placing a side panel onto the centre left panel, right sides facing, so that dots C are matching at the waistband and dots D at the hem. As before, first blanket stitch the edge then back stitch into the stitches below. Continue to attach all the side panels in the same way, working on either side of the central front panels – there should be four panels on either side of the centre line (see **Fig B**).

6 To sew up the back panels, place the edges of the outer side panels together, right sides facing, and pin. Starting at the asterisk, blanket stitch then back stitch the edge, working down to D (see **Fig C**).

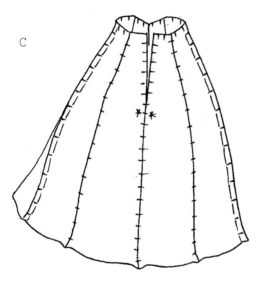

C

7 Turn the skirt the right side out. Blanket stitch around the entire waistband and back edges, then sew a hook and eye closure in place to reinforce the waistband.

SLIPPERS

1 Follow Steps 1 to 6 of the Shoes section from the Girls' Night Out project (see Girls' Night Out).

2 Now transfer dots A and B from the slipper top pattern piece onto the two pieces of felt you have cut for these. With metallic embroidery thread, blanket stitch around the toe ends from A to A then around the edges from B to B. Do not blanket stitch the short sides between A and B at this stage (see **Fig D**).

3 Sew seed beads onto the three dots marked just above the inside edge of each slipper top.

4 Position each slipper top onto its sole, aligning dots A on the slipper top with dots at A on the sole, then pin in place. Working from each dot A around to dot B, blanket stitch the slipper top onto the sole (see **Fig D**).

D

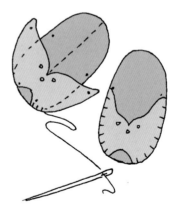

5 Use a cotton bud (Q-tip) to spread a fine layer of glue onto the tops of the slippers, being careful to avoid applying it to the beads. Sprinkle glitter onto the surfaces and allow it to dry then tap off any excess.

TIARA

1 To make the tiara, you'll need to cut two outer templates from felt. For the inner template, use a pencil to trace the pattern onto the bottom edge of an empty paper towel or toilet paper roll. Then cut out the template with a pair of sharp scissors – the curvature of the roll will help give the tiara its rounded shape. Now use your disappearing ink marker to transfer the additional markings shown on the patterns onto these felt and cardstock pieces.

2 Sew seed beads onto the dots on the front facing felt piece (see **Fig E**).

3 Using a cotton bud dipped in a small amount of glue, apply a thin coat of glue to the outer side of the inner tiara that you've cut out from cardstock.

4 Place the front facing felt piece in front of you, so that the wrong side of the felt is facing up, then position the inner cardstock piece onto its back with the glue facing down. Working from the centre outwards, gently press the cardboard piece onto the felt, making sure the cardboard is centred. You'll find that the inner cardboard tiara is slightly smaller than the felt outer one to make room for stitching the front and back felt pieces together later on (see **Fig E**).

5 Now apply a thin layer of glue onto the exposed cardstock. Stick the back facing felt piece onto the cardstock, making sure that the edges align with the front facing felt piece, then allow the glue to dry thoroughly.

6 Using metallic embroidery thread, blanket stitch around the entire edge of the tiara (see **Fig F**).

F

7 Finally, use your cotton bud to spread a fine layer of glue onto the front of the tiara, being careful to avoid applying it to the beads. Sprinkle glitter onto the surface and allow it to dry then tap off any excess.

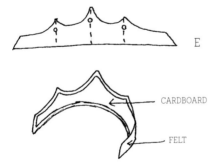

E

CARDBOARD

FELT

PATTERNS
Little Princess

Also use the patterns from the Basic Doll project (see How to Sew the Basic Doll).
All the patterns are actual size, so there is no need to enlarge or reduce them.

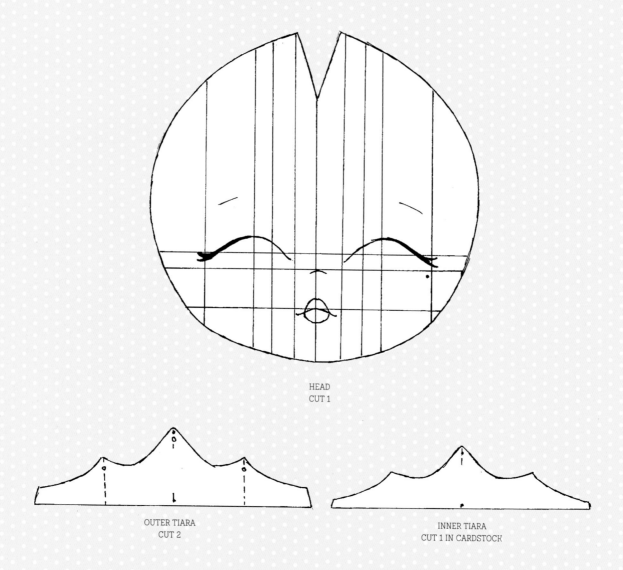

HEAD
CUT 1

OUTER TIARA
CUT 2

INNER TIARA
CUT 1 IN CARDSTOCK

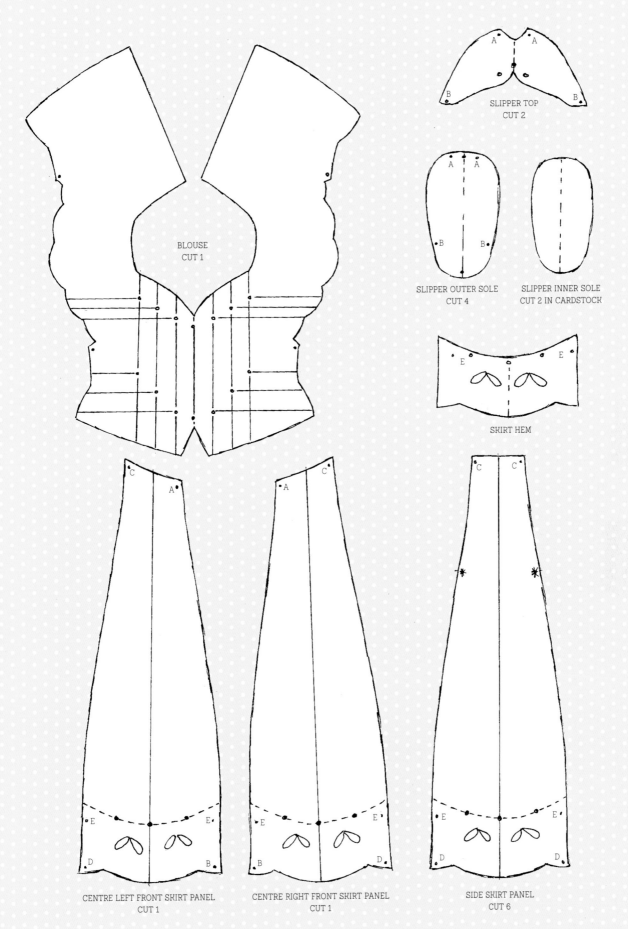

BLOUSE
CUT 1

SLIPPER TOP
CUT 2

SLIPPER OUTER SOLE
CUT 4

SLIPPER INNER SOLE
CUT 2 IN CARDSTOCK

SKIRT HEM

CENTRE LEFT FRONT SKIRT PANEL
CUT 1

CENTRE RIGHT FRONT SKIRT PANEL
CUT 1

SIDE SKIRT PANEL
CUT 6

BEDTIME Doll

IT'S BEEN A BUSY DAY AND THIS SWEET GIRL IS TRYING VERY HARD TO STAY AWAKE LONG ENOUGH FOR HER NIGHTLY BEDTIME STORY. DAD IS ALL SET TO TUCK HER AND HER LITTLE BEAR INTO HER COSY BED, WHERE SHE'LL DRIFT OFF TO SLEEP LISTENING TO HER FAVOURITE FAIRY TALE. SHE WEARS A PRETTY PAIR OF SUMMER PYJAMAS EDGED IN RUFFLED LACE, AND HER OH-SO-CUTE LITTLE BUNNY SLIPPERS ARE DELIGHTFULLY FUN AND EASY TO MAKE!

YOU WILL Need

- MATERIALS FOR THE BASIC DOLL PROJECT (SEE HOW TO SEW THE BASIC DOLL)
- SCRAPS OF FELT FOR THE FLOWER PETALS AND BODICE DETAILS
- ELASTIC LACE TRIM, 50CM (20IN) LENGTH
- SEAM BINDING FOR THE HAIR, 50CM (20IN) LENGTH, 6MM (¼IN) DIAMETER
- SEED BEADS • SMALL HOOK AND EYE CLOSURE • ONE SAFETY EYE, 4.5MM (³⁄₁₆IN) DIAMETER
- FRAY CHECK LIQUID • 5 X 15CM (2 X 6IN) CARDSTOCK FOR THE INNER SOLES OF THE SLIPPERS
- SEAM BINDING OR RIBBON IN TWO COLOURS, 10CM (4IN) IN LENGTH

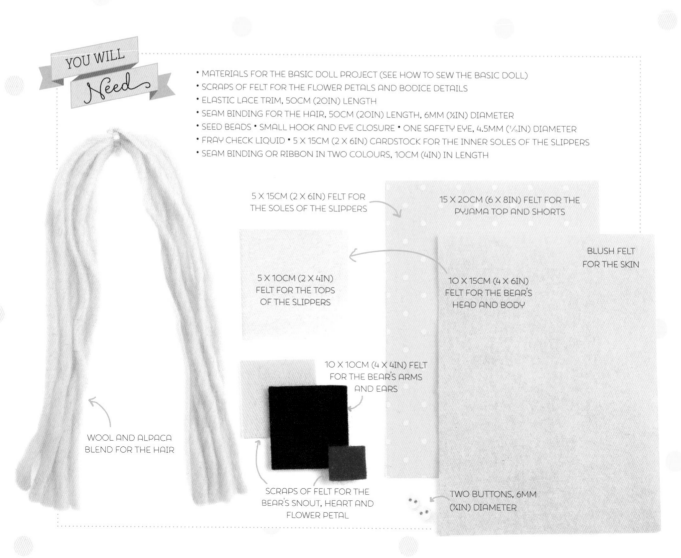

5 X 15CM (2 X 6IN) FELT FOR THE SOLES OF THE SLIPPERS

15 X 20CM (6 X 8IN) FELT FOR THE PYJAMA TOP AND SHORTS

5 X 10CM (2 X 4IN) FELT FOR THE TOPS OF THE SLIPPERS

BLUSH FELT FOR THE SKIN

10 X 15CM (4 X 6IN) FELT FOR THE BEAR'S HEAD AND BODY

10 X 10CM (4 X 4IN) FELT FOR THE BEAR'S ARMS AND EARS

WOOL AND ALPACA BLEND FOR THE HAIR

SCRAPS OF FELT FOR THE BEAR'S SNOUT, HEART AND FLOWER PETAL

TWO BUTTONS, 6MM (¼IN) DIAMETER

CUTTING AND ASSEMBLY

1 Follow the steps for making the Basic Doll up to Step 10 of the Hair section (see How to Sew the Basic Doll).

HAIR

1 To style the doll's hair, divide the strands into two ponytails, then fix each in place using a 25cm (10in) length of the 6mm (¼in) diameter seam binding.

PYJAMA TOP

1 Using your disappearing ink marker, first transfer all the dots, markings and ruled lines shown on the pyjama top front pattern onto the piece of felt you have cut for it.

2 Sew a button onto each of the two X markings on the front. Then position each decorative strip onto the marked lines on either side of the buttons. Using a tiny running stitch (see Stitch Guide), sew down the centre of each (see **Fig A**).

3 Now position each back piece against its corresponding front piece, wrong sides facing, and blanket stitch (see Stitch Guide) the shoulder seams together. Then blanket stitch around the entire neck opening and the inner edges of each back piece, as shown (see **Fig A**).

4 Measure the diameter of each armhole and cut a strip of lace to the length required for each one. Pin the lace to each armhole opening from the wrong side of the felt, then use tiny stitches to fix it in place (see **Fig A**). The lace will give the look of a pretty, frilly cap sleeve.

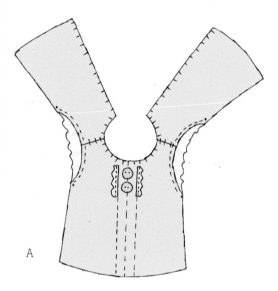

A

5 Whip stitch (see Stitch Guide) the side seams together, starting at the dot below each armhole and working down to the bottom edge of the top (see **Fig B**).

6 Measure the diameter of the bottom hem and cut a strip of lace to the length required. Pin the lace along the bottom hem from the wrong side of the felt then use tiny stitches to fix this in place (see **Fig B**).

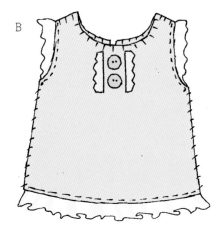

B

7 Stitch a hook and eye closure at the back of the pyjama top.

PYJAMA SHORTS

1 Place the piece of felt you have cut for the front of the shorts onto the back, wrong sides facing, and whip stitch the outer seams of the shorts together – also whip stitch around the central crotch area. Then use blanket stitch to sew around the entire waistband.

2 Measure the diameter of each leg opening and cut a strip of lace to the length required for each one. Pin the lace around each leg opening from the wrong side of the felt, then use tiny stitches to fix this in place (see **Fig C**).

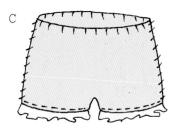

C

BUNNY SLIPPERS

1 To make one little bunny slipper, you'll need two soles cut from felt and one sole cut from cardstock, as well as a felt slipper top and flower petal. First, use your disappearing ink marker to transfer the dots, the X marking and the ruled lines shown on the patterns onto these felt pieces.

2 To make one slipper sole, squeeze a little blob of glue onto a scrap piece of paper, then use a cotton bud (Q-tip) to apply a thin layer to one side of the cardstock sole. Using the dots marked at the heel and toe as a guide for alignment, fix this slightly smaller cardstock sole on top of the outer felt sole.

3 Now apply a thin layer of glue onto the upper side of the cardstock sole and position the inner felt sole at the top of the pile, making sure everything is centred and the dots are aligned (see **Fig D**). Repeat with the second slipper and allow the glue on each to dry.

4 To finish both soles, simply blanket stitch around the edges of each (see **Fig E**).

D 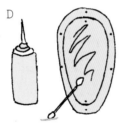 E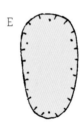

5 To complete your first slipper, now blanket stitch around the edges of a felt slipper top, from dot A just below the bunny's ear to dot B (see **Fig F**).

6 Embroider the eyes and nose of the bunny onto the slipper top. Then use your pink coloured pencil to add a bit of colour to the bunny's cheeks and inner ear areas.

7 Now position the slipper top onto the sole, aligning the dot at the centre of the slipper top with the dot at the centre of sole, and pin in place. Working from the centre dot around to dot B, blanket stitch the slipper top onto the sole, then repeat on the other side (see **Fig F**).

F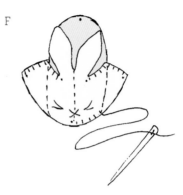

8 Position the flower petal just below an outer bunny ear and sew in place, stitching a little seed bead at the centre (see **Fig G**).

9 Repeat Steps 5 to 8 to complete your other slipper (see **Fig G**).

G

5 Use straight stitches (see Stitch Guide) to embroider a little X shape for the missing eye, then add a tiny eyelash at the outer corner of the safety eye, and eyebrows just above the bear's eyes (see **Fig H**).

6 Using your pink coloured pencil, introduce a bit of colour to the bear's cheeks. Then stitch the flower petal just above one eyebrow with a seed bead at its centre (see **Fig H**).

H

BEDTIME BEAR'S HEAD

1 With your disappearing ink marker, first transfer the markings from the bear patterns onto the head, snout and body felt pieces, using a ruler to connect the lines on the head and body.

2 Embroider a little nose on the snout. Then position the snout on the piece of felt you have cut for the bear's head and appliqué stitch (see Stitch Guide) this in place (see **Fig H**).

3 Being very careful, use the tip of the embroidery scissors or an awl to make a tiny hole for the eye at the centre of the smaller X (see **Fig H**), where the vertical and horizontal lines meet.

4 Insert a safety eye and connector at the back, making sure you slide the connector firmly down onto the post as far as it will go (see **Fig H**). Optional: once you've connected the eye parts, trim back the plastic posts of the safety eye with your wire cutters to leave about 4mm (⅛in) of post beyond the connectors.

7 Place the head front onto the head back, wrong sides facing, and pin together. Starting from the bottom, blanket stitch all the way around the head, leaving an opening for stuffing.

8 Stuff the bear's head firmly, then start to blanket stitch the opening closed. As you close the hole, add more stuffing if needed. The face should be full, rounded and quite firm, but not to the point of bursting at the seams. Leave a tail of thread (floss) for attaching the head to the body later.

BEDTIME BEAR'S EARS

1 Blanket stitch each of the bear's ears together, leaving an opening at the bottom to add a pinch of stuffing. Once you've added the stuffing, blanket stitch the opening closed.

2 Pin the ears in place on the head and ladder stitch (see Stitch Guide) the front and back of each ear to the head seam.

BEDTIME BEAR'S BODY

1 With a contrasting embroidery thread, use tiny stitches to transfer the dotted centre seam shown on the pattern onto the pieces of felt you have cut for the front and back of the bear's body (see **Fig H**).

2 Position the felt heart patch onto the front of the body and appliqué stitch this in place, adding a few straight stitches in black thread for detail (see **Fig H**).

3 Then embroider a few black stitches onto the back of the bear's body so they look like they're patching up a small tear in the seam (see **Fig I**).

4 Place the front body onto the back, wrong sides facing, then blanket stitch around the body, starting at one side of the neck. When you reach halfway up the body on the opposite side, stop stitching and add stuffing to the legs, before blanket stitching up to the other side of the neck.

5 Stuff the rest of the body firmly, then run a tiny gathering stitch (see Stitch Guide) just below the top edge of the neck opening. Gently tighten the thread to close the hole, adding more stuffing as you go to fill up the neck area. Stitch this area closed so you end up with a tight, rounded nub.

BEDTIME BEAR'S ARMS

1 Taking the two pieces of felt you cut for each arm, place them together with the wrong sides facing. Blanket stitch around them, leaving an opening at the back. Stuff the arms, then blanket stitch them closed.

ASSEMBLING THE BEAR

1 Follow Steps 1 to 5 for Attaching the Head to the Body, and Steps 1 to 2 of Attaching the Arms and Legs to the Body, from the Basic Doll project (see How to Sew the Basic Doll).

BEDTIME BEAR'S RUFFLE COLLAR

1 To make the ruffle collar, place one length of the seam binding on top of the other, fold this in half widthways, then run a tiny gathering stitch just below the top folded edge (see **Fig I**). Apply a small bead of Fray Check liquid to each cut end of the ribbon you have created to help prevent the edges from fraying, then allow this to dry completely.

2 Pin one end of the ribbon at the centre of the back neck area (see **Fig I**). Then gather the ribbon length and pin it around the neck of the bear, positioning the opposite end of the ribbon next to the first at the back of the neck.

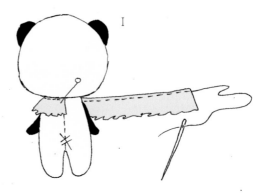

I

3 Sew the ruffle onto the neck with small stitches, inserting the needle in and out through the top area of the folded ruffle at the front and back of the neck to fix it in place.

PATTERNS
Bedtime Doll

Also use the patterns from the Basic Doll project (see How to Sew the Basic Doll).
All the patterns are actual size, so there is no need to enlarge or reduce them.

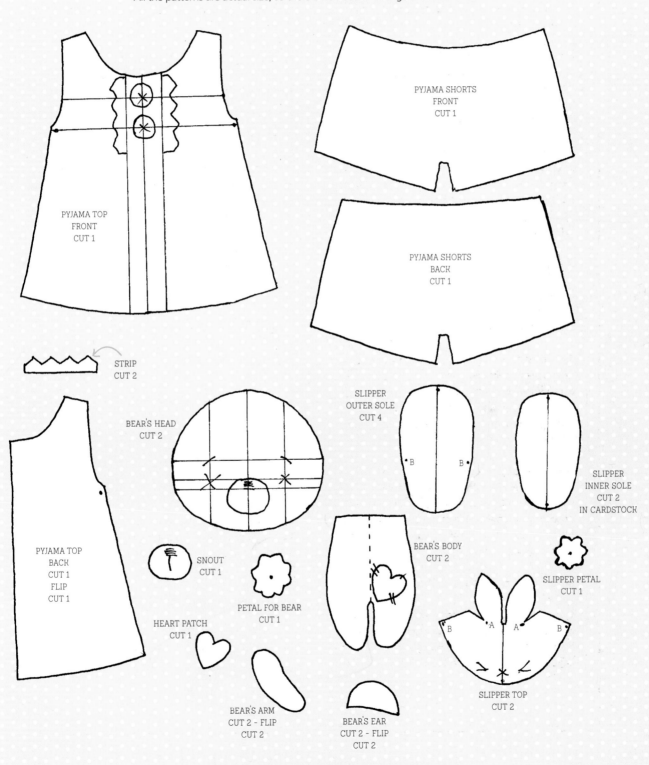

PYJAMA TOP
FRONT
CUT 1

PYJAMA SHORTS
FRONT
CUT 1

PYJAMA SHORTS
BACK
CUT 1

STRIP
CUT 2

BEAR'S HEAD
CUT 2

SLIPPER
OUTER SOLE
CUT 4

SLIPPER
INNER SOLE
CUT 2
IN CARDSTOCK

PYJAMA TOP
BACK
CUT 1
FLIP
CUT 1

SNOUT
CUT 1

BEAR'S BODY
CUT 2

SLIPPER PETAL
CUT 1

PETAL FOR BEAR
CUT 1

HEART PATCH
CUT 1

SLIPPER TOP
CUT 2

BEAR'S ARM
CUT 2 - FLIP
CUT 2

BEAR'S EAR
CUT 2 - FLIP
CUT 2

CIRCUS Ringmaster

"STEP RIGHT UP! WELCOME TO THE CIRCUS, THE GREATEST SHOW ON EARTH!" THIS CHARMING FELLOW, WITH HIS JAUNTY MOUSTACHE AND CHEERY FACE, IS ALL SET TO DAZZLE THE AUDIENCE ON THE BIG NIGHT. DRESSED IN HIS SCARLET TAILCOAT, DASHING TOP HAT AND CUMBERBUND TRIMMED WITH SPARKLING GLITTERED STARS, HE'S READY TO ANNOUNCE THE BEGINNING OF A MOST SPECTACULAR SHOW!

YOU WILL Need

- MATERIALS FOR THE BASIC DOLL PROJECT (SEE HOW TO SEW THE BASIC DOLL)
- EIGHT SEED BEADS FOR THE SHOES • GLITTER • FIVE SNAP CLOSURES, 5MM (¼IN) DIAMETER
- WHITE PAINT • FLAT TOOTHPICK
- COTTON BUD (Q-TIP) OR TOOTHPICK, 2.5CM (1IN) LENGTH CUT FROM THE CENTRE OF THE STICK

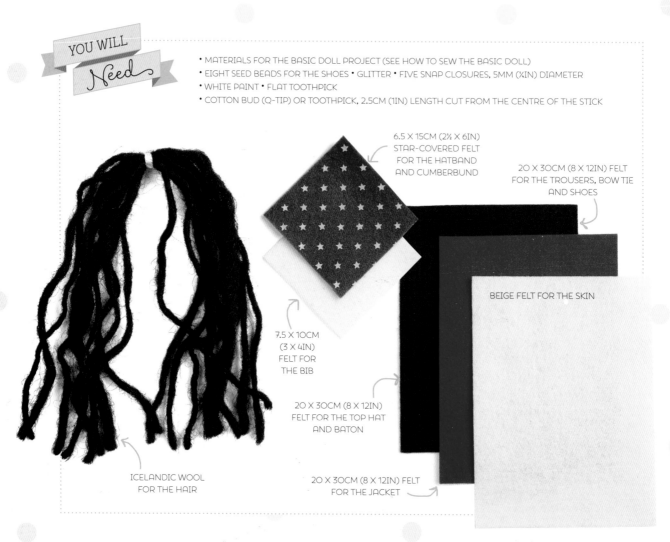

6.5 X 15CM (2½ X 6IN) STAR-COVERED FELT FOR THE HATBAND AND CUMBERBUND

20 X 30CM (8 X 12IN) FELT FOR THE TROUSERS, BOW TIE AND SHOES

7.5 X 10CM (3 X 4IN) FELT FOR THE BIB

BEIGE FELT FOR THE SKIN

20 X 30CM (8 X 12IN) FELT FOR THE TOP HAT AND BATON

ICELANDIC WOOL FOR THE HAIR

20 X 30CM (8 X 12IN) FELT FOR THE JACKET

CUTTING AND ASSEMBLY

1 Follow the steps for making the Basic Doll up to Step 4 of the Layout and Cutting section (see How to Sew the Basic Doll), using the head and body pattern pieces provided for this project instead of the Basic Doll.

HEAD

1 With your disappearing ink marker, transfer the facial markings shown on the head pattern onto the piece of felt you have cut out for it.

2 Using the placement guide, position the moustache just below the nose so it is centred on the marked line, then appliqué stitch (see Stitch Guide) this in place. In the same way, position the eyebrows, then appliqué stitch them in place too.

3 Using stem stitch (see Stitch Guide), embroider the mouth just below the moustache.

4 Follow Steps 3 to 6 for making the Head (see How to Sew the Basic Doll), omitting to embroider the eyelashes and eyebrows on the face.

ASSEMBLING THE BASIC DOLL

1 Follow the steps for making the Basic Doll from Step 1 of the Assembling the Head section up to Step 9 of the Hair section (see How to Sew the Basic Doll).

HAIR

1 To style the doll's hair carefully trim the ends, starting at the centre back and working out to each side, then cut a fringe.

JACKET

1 Using your disappearing ink marker, first transfer all the dots and the ruled lines shown on the jacket patterns onto the felt pieces you have cut for them.

2 Pin the collar onto the jacket, aligning the dots. Starting at the dot at the back of the neck, blanket stitch (see Stitch Guide) around and down one side of

the collar and then the hem of the jacket. Repeat on the opposite side (see **Fig A**).

3 From the wrong side of the fabric, next whip stitch (see Stitch Guide) the darts together (see **Fig A**).

A
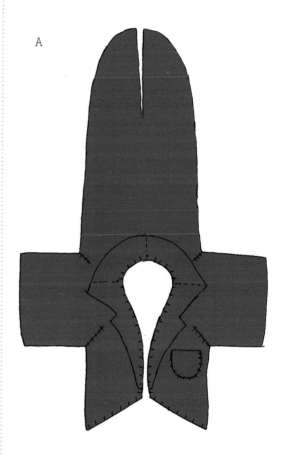

4 Now position the pocket onto the front side of the jacket and pin. Use appliqué stitch to sew it in place, leaving the top edge of the pocket open (see **Fig A**).

5 Fold the jacket in half, matching the body and sleeve edges together, then whip stitch these side edges together (see **Fig B**).

6 To create the illusion of a little handkerchief peeping out of the jacket pocket, cut a couple of tiny scrap triangles from leftover bits of the same felt used to make the decorative hat band or cumberbund, then insert them into the pocket of the jacket (see **Fig B**).

B

TROUSERS

1 From the back of the felt, whip stitch the darts together on the front and back trouser pieces. Then place the front piece onto the back, wrong sides facing, and whip stitch first the outer seams then the inner ones together (see **Fig C**).

2 Fit the trousers on the doll, with the slit at the back of his body – you should be able to overlap one side of the waistband over the other. Determine where to fix a snap closure, then remove the trousers from the doll and sew it in place (see **Fig C**).

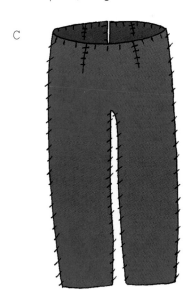

C

BIB

1 Using your disappearing ink marker, first transfer the X marking shown on the bib pattern onto the felt piece you have cut for it.

2 Fold the corners of the jacket collar over and gently press them with a warm iron.

3 Position the bow tie just below the collar on the X marking, then sew the centre of the bow in place (see **Fig D**).

4 Fit the bib on your doll, wrapping the long ends around the neck to overlap so you can see where to attach the snap closure. Sew this in place (see **Fig D**).

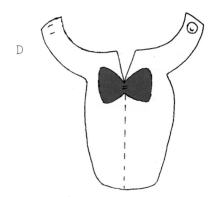

D

TOP HAT

1 Place both of the brim pieces on top of each other and pin them. Then blanket stitch around the outer edge to create a sturdy brim (see **Fig E**).

2 Now whip stitch the short sides of the hatband together. Centre and pin the crown at the top, then blanket stitch all the way around to fix this to the hatband (see **Fig E**).

3 Position the open bottom edge of the hatband onto the inner opening of the hat brim and whip stitch them together (see **Fig E**).

4 Pin the decorative band onto the hatband, aligning the short sides with the whip-stitched seam of the hatband – the bottom long edge of the decorative band should be perfectly aligned with the whip-stitched seam where the brim joins the band. Whip stitch the short sides of the band together, then use tiny stitches to fix the band in place just inside each long edge (see **Fig E**).

E

5 Apply a tiny dab of glue to each star on the decorative felt band with a flat toothpick and sprinkle a tiny bit of glitter onto each. Allow it to dry then gently tap off any excess glitter.

SHOES

1 Using your disappearing ink marker, first transfer the dots, the X marking and the ruled lines shown on the front and sole patterns of the shoes onto the felt pieces you have cut for them.

2 To make one shoe, sew a seed bead onto each dot marked on the top piece, then use contrasting embroidery thread (floss) to embroider an X shape between them (see **Fig F**).

3 Fold the shoe top in half and whip stitch the back ends together, then blanket stitch around the inner edge of the shoe top (see **Fig F**).

4 Place the felt piece you cut for the sole onto the bottom of the shoe top, aligning the dots at the heel and toe, then blanket stitch the sole onto the shoe top (see **Fig F**).

5 Fit the shoe onto the doll. Place the strap over the top of the shoe, position the narrow end on the side of the shoe top and stitch it in place. Embroider a tiny buckle at the wider end, then sew the male side of the snap closure underneath and the female side onto the side of the shoe top (see **Fig F**).

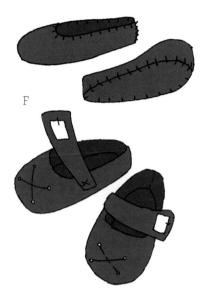

F

6 Repeat Steps 1 to 5 to make the other shoe.

CUMBERBUND

1 Sew a snap closure onto the narrow ends of the piece of felt for the cumberbund, then fit this on the doll.

BATON

1 Fold the piece of felt you cut for the baton in half lengthways. Then whip stitch around this, starting at the short straight edge and working around until just before the other rounded end. Insert the cut cotton bud (Q-tip) or toothpick into the tube for stability then continue whip stitching around to close (see **Fig G**).

2 Dip the rounded end of the baton into white paint to cover up to 4mm (⅛in) of the tip. Sprinkle the painted tip with glitter and tap off any excess (see **Fig G**), then allow to dry thoroughly.

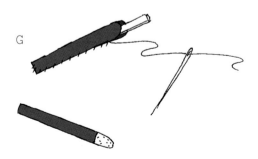

G

PATTERNS
Circus Ringmaster

Also use the patterns from the Basic Doll project (see How to Sew the Basic Doll).
All the patterns are actual size, so there is no need to enlarge or reduce them.

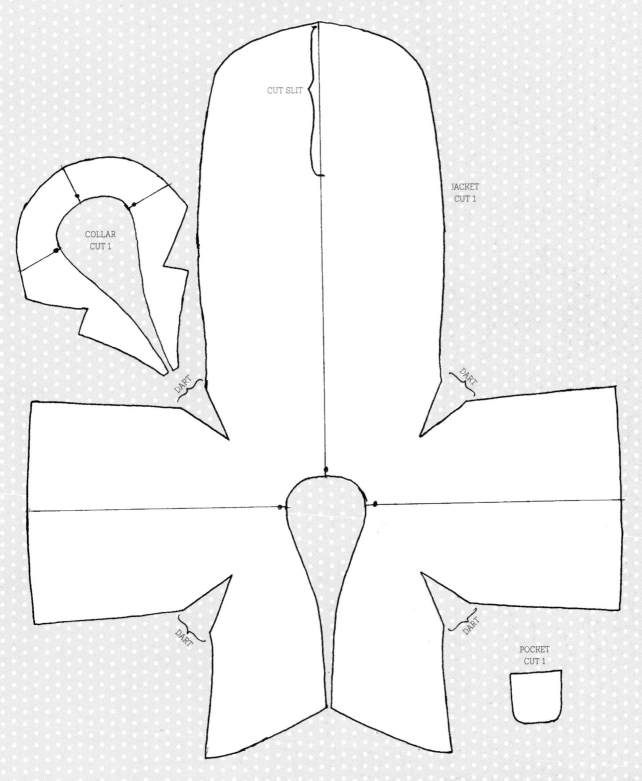

CUT SLIT

JACKET
CUT 1

COLLAR
CUT 1

DART

DART

DART

DART

POCKET
CUT 1

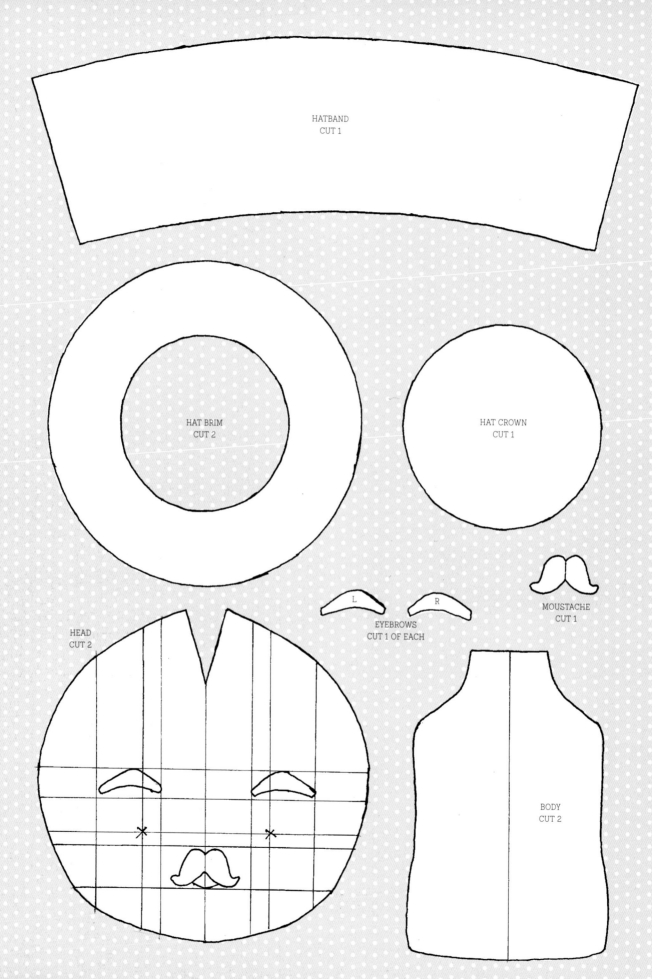

HATBAND
CUT 1

HAT BRIM
CUT 2

HAT CROWN
CUT 1

MOUSTACHE
CUT 1

HEAD
CUT 2

L   R
EYEBROWS
CUT 1 OF EACH

BODY
CUT 2

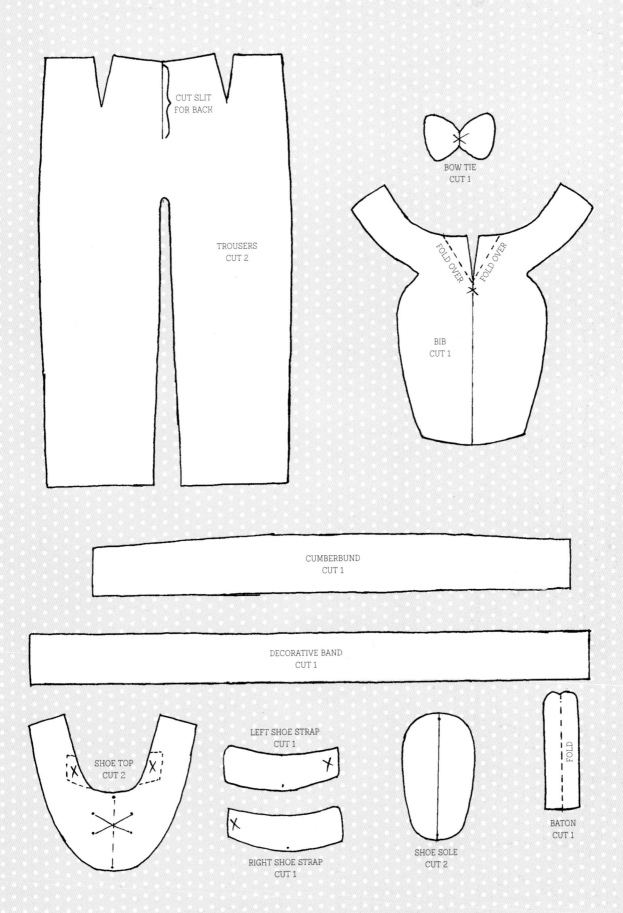

CUT SLIT
FOR BACK

TROUSERS
CUT 2

BOW TIE
CUT 1

FOLD OVER   FOLD OVER

BIB
CUT 1

CUMBERBUND
CUT 1

DECORATIVE BAND
CUT 1

SHOE TOP
CUT 2

LEFT SHOE STRAP
CUT 1

RIGHT SHOE STRAP
CUT 1

SHOE SOLE
CUT 2

FOLD

BATON
CUT 1

LITTLE *Traveller*

WITH HER SUITCASE PACKED, THIS SWEET GIRL IS READY FOR AN ADVENTURE!
SHE'S OFF TO VISIT HER DEAR GRANNY OVER THE SUMMER HOLIDAYS,
AND CANNOT WAIT FOR THE JOURNEY TO BEGIN. SHE WEARS A PRETTY
EMBROIDERED DRESS WITH LACE AND BEAD TRIM, AND A DARLING LITTLE
JACKET TO WARD OFF ANY CHILLY BREEZES. BON VOYAGE LITTLE ONE!

YOU WILL *Need*

- MATERIALS FOR THE BASIC DOLL PROJECT (SEE HOW TO SEW THE BASIC DOLL)
- LACE TRIM FOR THE DRESS, 16.5CM (6½IN) LENGTH • SEED BEADS
- SMALL HOOK AND EYE CLOSURE FOR THE DRESS • THREE BUTTONS FOR THE JACKET, 6MM (¼IN) DIAMETER
- TWO BUTTONS FOR THE SHOES, 6MM (¼IN) DIAMETER
- TWO SNAP CLOSURES FOR THE SHOES, 5MM (⅛IN) DIAMETER
- 10 X 15CM (4 X 6IN) CARDSTOCK FOR THE INNER SUITCASE

10 X 15CM (4 X 6IN) FELT FOR THE SHOES

10 X 10CM (4 X 4IN) FELT FOR THE SUITCASE HANDLE

20 X 30CM (8 X 12IN) FELT FOR THE JACKET

TAN FELT FOR THE SKIN

SCRAPS OF FELT FOR THE SUITCASE NAME TAGS

10 X 15CM (4 X 6IN) FELT FOR THE SUITCASE

SPORT WOOL (YARN) FOR MAIN HAIR COLOUR, AND WOOL, ALPACA AND SILK BLEND FOR THE PALE PINK STREAKS

12.5 X 15CM (5 X 6IN) FELT FOR THE DRESS

CUTTING AND ASSEMBLY

1 Follow the steps for making the Basic Doll up to Step 3 of the Hair section (see How to Sew the Basic Doll).

HAIR

1 To create the look of highlights around the front hairline, add a few strands of pale pink wool (yarn) to the doll's hair before stitching it onto the head. Then continue with Steps 4 to 10 of the Hair section (see How to Sew the Basic Doll).

2 To style the doll's hair, gather it at the back of the head then tie it in place with ribbon.

JACKET

1 Using your disappearing ink marker, first transfer all the ruled lines shown on the jacket patterns onto the felt pieces you have cut for them.

2 Pin the collar on the jacket neckline, aligning the ruled lines, then blanket stitch (see Stitch Guide) this in place (see **Fig A**).

3 Now position the pocket onto the front of the jacket and pin. Sew this in place with tiny stitches, keeping these about 4mm (⅛in) away from the pocket edge, and leave the top edge of the pocket open (see **Fig A**).

4 Fold the jacket in half with the right sides facing, matching the front and sleeve edges together, then pin. Back stitch (see Stitch Guide) the side edges together, again keeping the stitches about 4mm (⅛in) away from the cut edge.

5 Using your embroidery scissors, carefully cut a few small notches into the curve of the fabric at the underarm, being careful not to cut into the stitches. Then turn the jacket the right way round and gently press.

6 Finally, sew three tiny buttons at the front of the jacket (see **Fig A**).

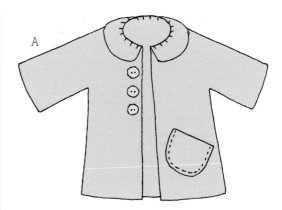

A

DRESS

1 Using your disappearing ink marker, first transfer all the dots, X markings for your embroidered details, and the ruled lines shown on the dress pattern onto the felt pieces you have cut for it.

2 Using three contrasting shades of embroidery thread (floss), stitch each row of X details (see **Fig B**).

3 Lay the front piece of the dress onto the back piece, wrong sides facing, then blanket stitch the shoulder seams together (see **Fig B**).

4 Whip stitch (see Stitch Guide) the side seams together, starting at the dot below each armhole and working down towards the bottom edge of the dress (see **Fig B**).

5 Now blanket stitch around the entire neckline, as well as each armhole (see **Fig B**). This will reinforce these openings and prevent them from warping when you are dressing the doll.

6 Sew a hook and eye closure at the back of the neck opening. Cut a length of lace trim to fit around the hem and pin it, then use tiny straight stitches (see Stitch Guide) to sew it in place. To finish, accentuate the trim by adding some seed beads above (see **Fig B**).

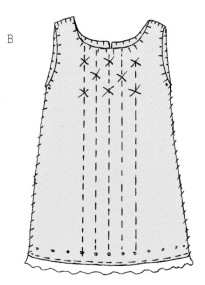

B

SHOES

1 Follow Steps 1 to 5 of the Shoes section from the Woodland Maiden project (see Woodland Maiden).

SUITCASE

1 Using your disappearing ink marker, first transfer the markings on the suitcase side pattern B onto the two felt pieces you have cut for this. Then transfer the illustrations on each of the travel sticker patterns and the name tag onto the pieces of felt you have cut for these, too.

2 Position the travel stickers onto the front and back A pieces (see **Fig C**), then use a contrasting thread to blanket stitch around the edge of each. Embroider the details onto each travel sticker using tiny back stitches.

3 Gather all the felt and cardstock pieces for the body of the suitcase, then lay them out so the wrong side of each felt piece is facing up on your workspace. Using a cotton bud (Q-tip), apply a thin layer of glue to one side of each card piece, then centre and stick it to its co-ordinating piece of felt – A on A, B on B, C on C. Allow the glue to dry thoroughly – the cardstock will help maintain the suitcase shape once it's been stuffed.

4 Prepare to sew the body of the suitcase together by facing all the cardstock inwards and the felt pieces outwards. Blanket stitch the long edge of B onto the long edge of A, and repeat by sewing the other long edge of B to the opposite long edge of A. Then blanket stitch the long edge of C to the short edge of A, and repeat by sewing the second long edge of C to the opposite short side of A. Blanket stitch together the short edges of B and C at each corner (see **Fig C**).

5 Position the second side A onto the suitcase, cardstock facing inwards. Now blanket stitch around the edges, leaving a small opening at the end. Use this opening to add stuffing to fill out the suitcase, then blanket stitch the opening closed (see **Fig C**).

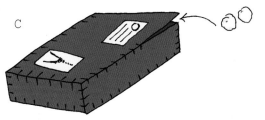

C

6 To make one handle, place two of the pieces of felt you cut for these together and blanket stitch around the inner and outer edges, leaving a piece of thread from the outer blanket stitches to sew the handles onto the suitcase later. Repeat this process for the second handle.

7 Pin the handles onto the top of the suitcase between the marked lines. Then use the thread left over from Step 6 to ladder stitch (see Stitch Guide) the bottom edges of each handle to the top of the suitcase.

8 On the front piece of name tag felt, use contrasting thread to embroider the rectangle frame, and black to embroider the little lines inside the frame. Place the front and back pieces together, then blanket stitch around the edges in a contrasting thread.

9 To finish, thread a needle through the dot on the name tag with a strand of silver embroidery thread and use this to tie it around one of the suitcase handles (see **Fig D**).

D

PATTERNS
Little Traveller

Also use the patterns from the Basic Doll project (see How to Sew the Basic Doll).
All the patterns are actual size, so there is no need to enlarge or reduce them.

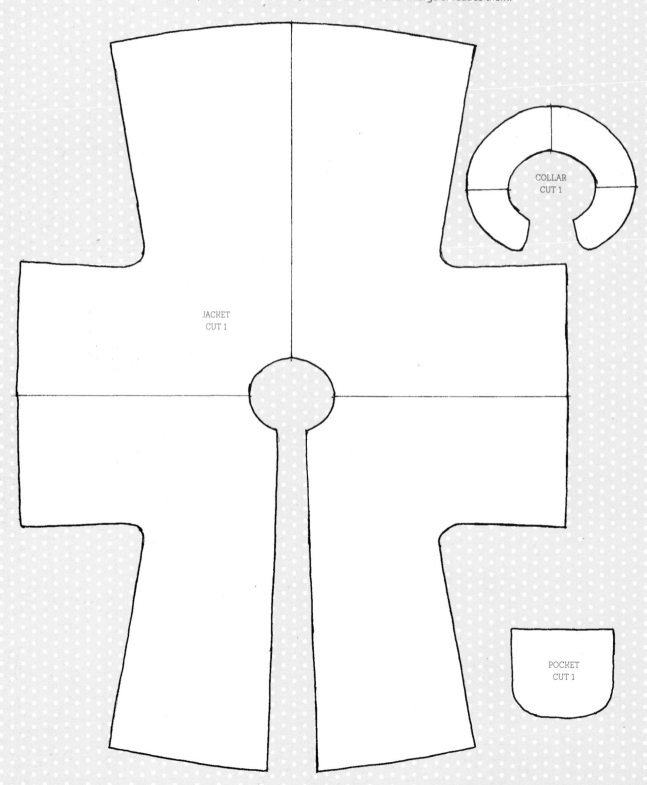

COLLAR
CUT 1

JACKET
CUT 1

POCKET
CUT 1

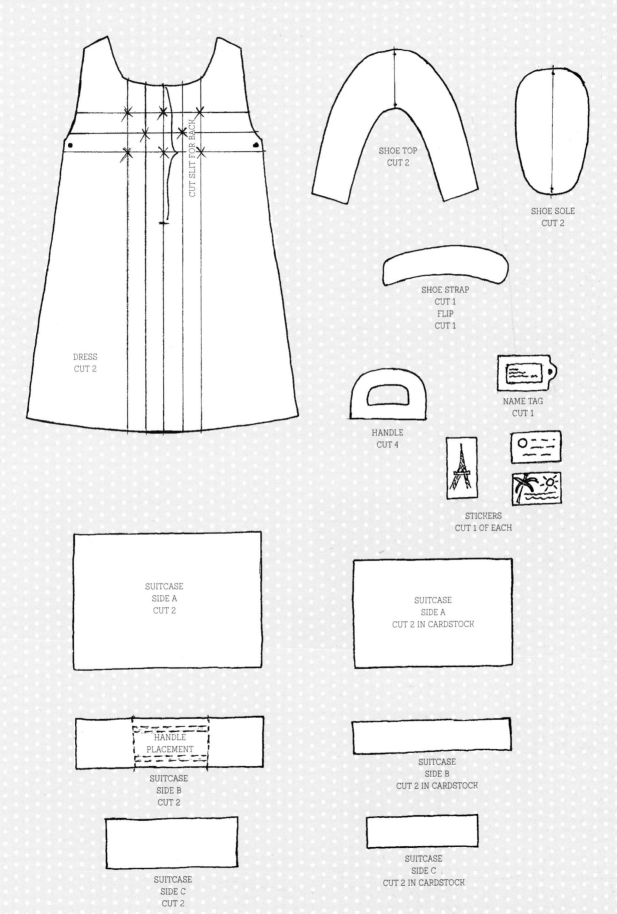

DRESS
CUT 2

CUT SLIT FOR BACK

SHOE TOP
CUT 2

SHOE SOLE
CUT 2

SHOE STRAP
CUT 1
FLIP
CUT 1

HANDLE
CUT 4

NAME TAG
CUT 1

STICKERS
CUT 1 OF EACH

SUITCASE
SIDE A
CUT 2

SUITCASE
SIDE A
CUT 2 IN CARDSTOCK

HANDLE
PLACEMENT

SUITCASE
SIDE B
CUT 2

SUITCASE
SIDE B
CUT 2 IN CARDSTOCK

SUITCASE
SIDE C
CUT 2

SUITCASE
SIDE C
CUT 2 IN CARDSTOCK

CUTE
Schoolgirl

HOPSCOTCH AND MARBLES, HISTORY AND MATHS – ALL THE THINGS THAT MAKE UP A BUSY DAY AT SCHOOL! THIS SWEET DOLL IS READY FOR THE FIRST CLASS OF THE DAY DRESSED IN A PRETTY PLAID SKIRT, BLAZER AND TIE, WITH WHITE ANKLE SOCKS AND BLACK MARY JANE SHOES. AN EXERCISE BOOK IN WHICH SHE PRACTISES HER WRITING IS TUCKED INTO AN ADORABLE SATCHEL THAT COMPLETES HER OUTFIT.

YOU WILL Need

- MATERIALS FOR THE BASIC DOLL PROJECT (SEE HOW TO SEW THE BASIC DOLL)
- 7.5 X 15CM (3 X 6IN) JERSEY FABRIC FOR THE SOCKS • LACE TRIM FOR THE SOCKS, 10CM (4IN) LENGTH
- BLACK SEAM BINDING FOR THE HAIR RIBBONS, 50CM (20IN) LENGTH, 1CM (¼IN) DIAMETER
- TWO SEED BEADS FOR THE SATCHEL • FIVE SNAP CLOSURES, 5MM (¼IN) DIAMETER
- TWO SMALL HOOK AND EYE CLOSURES FOR THE BLOUSE
- TWO BUTTONS FOR THE SHOES, 5MM (¼IN) DIAMETER

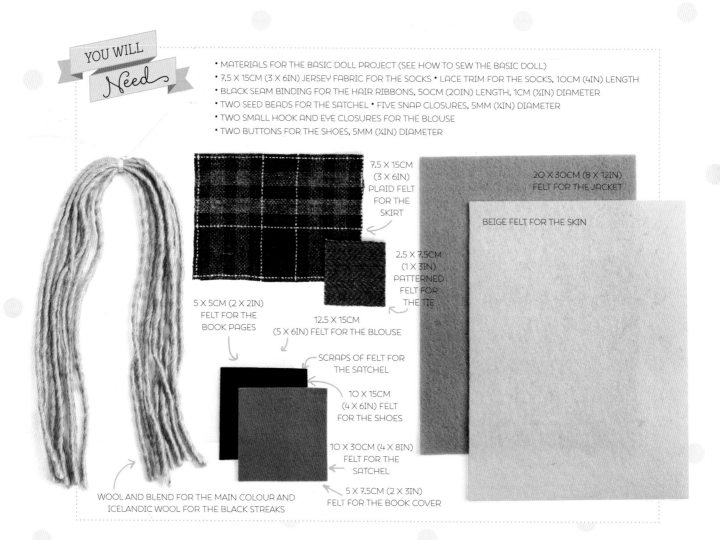

7.5 X 15CM (3 X 6IN) PLAID FELT FOR THE SKIRT

20 X 30CM (8 X 12IN) FELT FOR THE JACKET

BEIGE FELT FOR THE SKIN

2.5 X 7.5CM (1 X 3IN) PATTERNED FELT FOR THE TIE

5 X 5CM (2 X 2IN) FELT FOR THE BOOK PAGES

12.5 X 15CM (5 X 6IN) FELT FOR THE BLOUSE

SCRAPS OF FELT FOR THE SATCHEL

10 X 15CM (4 X 6IN) FELT FOR THE SHOES

10 X 30CM (4 X 8IN) FELT FOR THE SATCHEL

5 X 7.5CM (2 X 3IN) FELT FOR THE BOOK COVER

WOOL AND BLEND FOR THE MAIN COLOUR AND ICELANDIC WOOL FOR THE BLACK STREAKS

LAYOUT AND CUTTING

1 Follow the steps for making the Basic Doll up to Step 1 of the Head section (see How to Sew the Basic Doll), using the head pattern provided for this project instead of the Basic Doll.

HEAD

1 With your disappearing ink marker, transfer the facial markings shown on the head pattern onto the piece of felt you have cut for out for it.

2 In addition, cut out the paper templates for the glasses frames. With your disappearing ink marker, trace each frame onto the front of the face, using the grid on the face template as your guide for placement, then draw a connecting bridge between the two frames over the nose area.

3 Using one strand of embroidery thread (floss), outline the glasses frames with stem stitch (see Stitch Guide).

4 Follow Steps 2 to 6 for making the Head (see How to Sew the Basic Doll).

ASSEMBLY OF THE BASIC DOLL

1 Follow the steps for making the Basic Doll from Step 1 of the Assembling the Head section up to Step 3 of the Hair section (see How to Sew the Basic Doll).

HAIR

1 Add a strand of contrasting wool (yarn) – for my doll, I used black – into the doll's hair before stitching it onto the head. Then continue with Steps 4 to 10 of the Hair section (see How to Sew the Basic Doll).

2 To style the doll's hair, divide it into two ponytails, tied at each side of the head with black seam binding.

JACKET

1 Using your disappearing ink marker, first transfer all the dots and the ruled lines shown on the jacket patterns onto the felt pieces you have cut for them.

2 Pin the collar onto the jacket, aligning the dots, then blanket stitch (see Stitch Guide) this in place (see **Fig A**).

3 Using stem stitch and one strand of embroidery thread, embroider the crest on the pocket. Position the pocket on the front side of the jacket and pin, then use appliqué stitch (see Stitch Guide) to sew this in place, leaving the top edge open (see **Fig A**).

4 From the wrong side of the fabric, whip stitch the darts together (see **Fig A**).

A
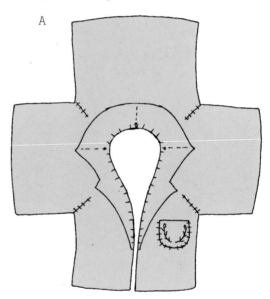

5 Fold the jacket in half, matching the front and sleeve edges together, then whip stitch the side edges together (see **Fig B**).

B

SKIRT

1 If you'd like to accentuate the plaid pattern on the skirt, use a tiny running stitch (see Stitch Guide) and a metallic or contrasting embroidery thread to accentuate the vertical and horizontal lines of the plaid felt.

2 From the wrong side of the fabric, whip stitch the darts together (see **Fig C**).

3 Using a contrasting embroidery thread, blanket stitch around the waist edge and sides of the skirt (see **Fig C**).

4 Fit the skirt on the doll, wrapping it around her so that the sides overlap at the back. Determine where to attach the two snap closures, then sew these in place (see **Fig C**).

C

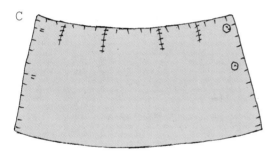

BLOUSE AND TIE

1 Using your disappearing ink marker, first transfer all the markings shown on the blouse patterns onto the felt pieces you have cut for it.

2 Position each side of the collar onto the neckline of the blouse, aligning the asterisks on the collar with the asterisks on the neckline of the blouse, then blanket stitch in place (see **Fig D**).

3 Fold the tie in half. Then position it centrally at the opening of the collar at the front of the blouse and sew it in place using a few tiny stitches (see **Fig D**).

4 Position the pocket onto the front of the blouse and pin. Appliqué stitch this in place, leaving the top edge open (see **Fig D**).

D

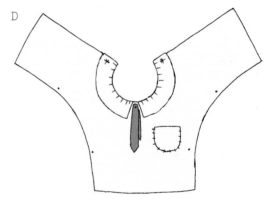

5 Fold the blouse in half at the shoulders, matching the front and back together, with wrong sides facing. Then whip stitch the side seams together, starting at the dot below each armhole and working down to the hem (see **Fig E**).

6 Now blanket stitch around the hems and armholes of the blouse (see **Fig E**). This will reinforce these openings and prevent them from warping when you are dressing the doll.

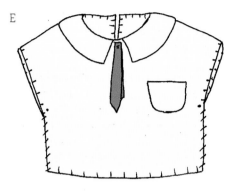

E

7 To finish, sew the two hook and eye closures onto the back of the blouse.

SOCKS

1 Follow Steps 1 to 5 of the Socks section from the Woodland Maiden project (see Woodland Maiden).

SHOES

1 Follow Steps 1 to 5 of the Shoes section from the Woodland Maiden project (see Woodland Maiden).

SATCHEL

1 Using your disappearing ink marker, first transfer the markings shown on both the front and back satchel patterns to both the right and wrong sides of the pieces of felt you have cut for them.

2 Sew a seed bead onto the dot marked on each satchel tab. Then position the tabs over the markings at the top of the right side of the back satchel piece and sew in place with tiny stitches (see **Fig F**).

F

3 Now turn the satchel back piece over so that the wrong side is facing you. Align one end of the gusset piece with the dot halfway down the left-hand side of the satchel back, then whip stitch the edge of the gusset onto the bottom edge of the satchel. Work around to the opposite side of the satchel, making sure the centre line of the gusset is aligned with the centre line of the satchel back (see **Fig G**).

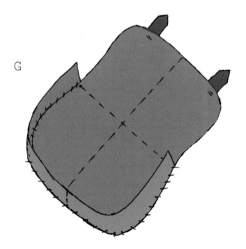

G

4 Sew the female side of a snap closure onto the right side of the satchel front at the X marking. Then sew the male side onto the wrong side of the satchel back at the X marking (see **Fig H**).

5 Position the satchel front onto the curved edge of the gusset, aligning the centre line on each, then whip stitch around the sides and bottom to fix this in place (see **Fig H**).

6 Insert about 4mm (⅛in) of one strap end into the inside of the gusset area and sew in place with a few tiny stitches. Sew the female side of a snap closure on the outside of the gusset, at the opposite side of the bag. Then sew the male side of the snap closure onto the opposite end of the strap (see **Fig H**). This will allow you to cross the satchel over the doll's body easily.

H

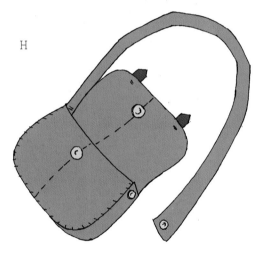

EXERCISE BOOK

1 Using your disappearing ink marker, first transfer the letters A, B and C onto one of the felt book pages, then use back stitch (see Stitch Guide) and one strand of embroidery thread to embroider these letters in place.

2 Position the page with the embroidered letters onto the second felt page and then use tiny stitches to sew the left-hand side of the pages together very close to the edge.

3 Using your disappearing ink marker, now transfer all the dots and asterisks shown on the book cover pattern onto both the right and wrong sides of the felt piece you have cut for it. Then use a ruler to connect the dots down the centre of the book.

4 Lay the pages of the book onto the inside of the book cover, wrong side facing up, just to the right of the centre line. Insert a needle threaded with one strand of contrasting embroidery thread, knotted at the end, through the top asterisk from the inside of the book cover and out through to the other side (see **Fig I**).

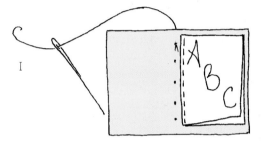

I

5 Close the book, making sure the inner pages are aligned with the edges of the outer book cover. Use the embroidery thread from Step 4 to blanket stitch down the entire spine of the book, using the asterisks as your stitch guide (see **Fig J**). Your stitches should be long enough to go through the pages inside the book so they are secure and unable to slip out. The book will fit nicely into the satchel.

J

PATTERNS
Cute Schoolgirl

Also use the patterns from the Basic Doll project (see How to Sew the Basic Doll).
All the patterns are actual size, so there is no need to enlarge or reduce them.

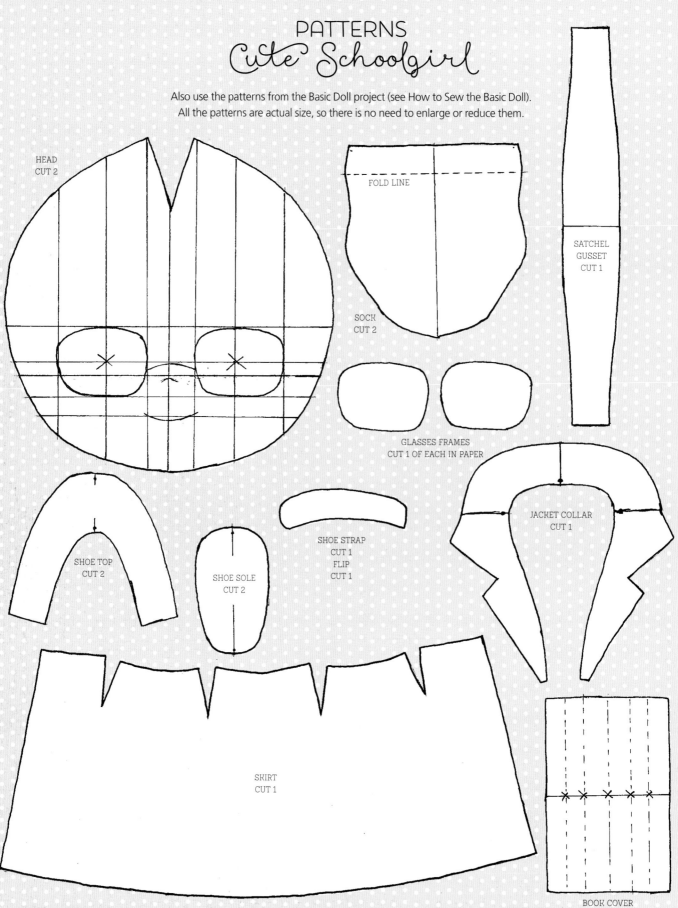

HEAD
CUT 2

FOLD LINE

SATCHEL
GUSSET
CUT 1

SOCK
CUT 2

GLASSES FRAMES
CUT 1 OF EACH IN PAPER

JACKET COLLAR
CUT 1

SHOE TOP
CUT 2

SHOE SOLE
CUT 2

SHOE STRAP
CUT 1
FLIP
CUT 1

SKIRT
CUT 1

BOOK COVER
CUT 1

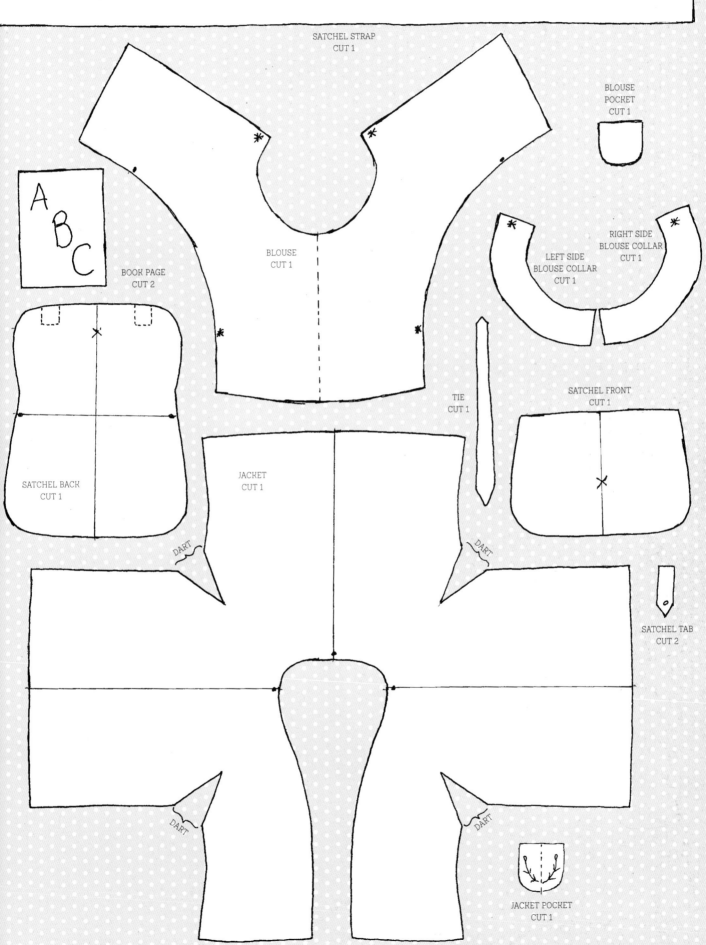

SATCHEL STRAP
CUT 1

BLOUSE
POCKET
CUT 1

A B C

BOOK PAGE
CUT 2

BLOUSE
CUT 1

LEFT SIDE
BLOUSE COLLAR
CUT 1

RIGHT SIDE
BLOUSE COLLAR
CUT 1

TIE
CUT 1

SATCHEL FRONT
CUT 1

SATCHEL BACK
CUT 1

JACKET
CUT 1

DART

DART

SATCHEL TAB
CUT 2

DART

DART

JACKET POCKET
CUT 1

WOODLAND *Maiden*

A LOVER OF NATURE, THIS SWEET LITTLE MAIDEN CAN OFTEN BE
FOUND WANDERING THROUGH THE WOODS WITH HER SMALL
BASKET, COLLECTING FLOWERS AND OTHER TINY TREASURES
AS SHE ADMIRES HER WONDERFUL SURROUNDINGS.

YOU WILL *Need*

- MATERIALS FOR THE BASIC DOLL PROJECT (SEE HOW TO SEW THE BASIC DOLL)
- 7.5 X 15CM (3 X 6IN) JERSEY FABRIC FOR THE SOCKS • SEAM BINDING FOR THE BONNET TIES, 1CM (⅜IN) WIDTH
- LACE TRIM FOR THE DRESS AND SOCKS, 28CM (11IN) LENGTH
- NARROW RIBBON FOR THE HAIR, 36CM (14IN) LENGTH • SMALL HOOK AND EYE CLOSURE FOR THE CAPE
- TWO BUTTONS FOR THE DRESS STRAPS, 6MM (¼IN) DIAMETER • AWL
- FOUR SNAP CLOSURES FOR THE DRESS AND BLOUSE, 5MM (³⁄₁₆IN) DIAMETER • FRAY CHECK LIQUID
- TWO BLACK SEED BEADS FOR THE HEDGEHOG'S EYES • PINK COLOURED PENCIL
- COLOURED FELT OR FINE MARKER PENS • STUFFING • COCKTAIL (ORANGE) STICK

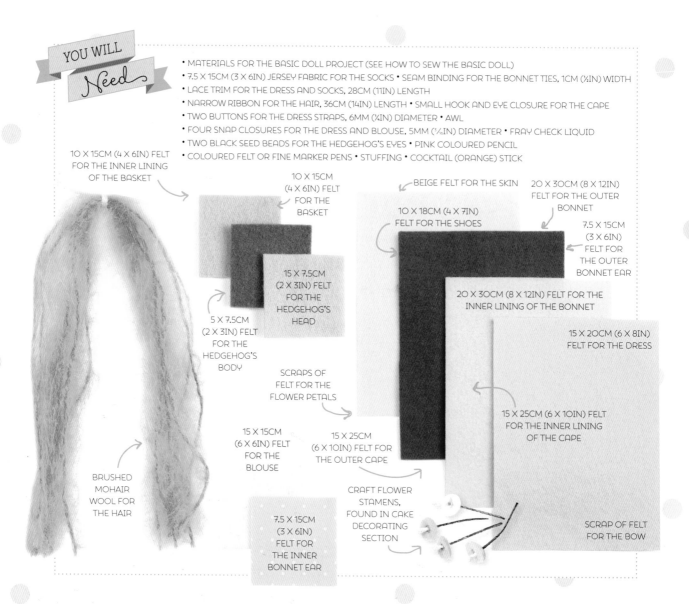

10 X 15CM (4 X 6IN) FELT
FOR THE INNER LINING
OF THE BASKET

10 X 15CM
(4 X 6IN) FELT
FOR THE
BASKET

BEIGE FELT FOR THE SKIN

20 X 30CM (8 X 12IN)
FELT FOR THE OUTER
BONNET

10 X 18CM (4 X 7IN)
FELT FOR THE SHOES

7.5 X 15CM
(3 X 6IN)
FELT FOR
THE OUTER
BONNET EAR

15 X 7.5CM
(2 X 3IN) FELT
FOR THE
HEDGEHOG'S
HEAD

20 X 30CM (8 X 12IN) FELT FOR THE
INNER LINING OF THE BONNET

5 X 7.5CM
(2 X 3IN) FELT
FOR THE
HEDGEHOG'S
BODY

15 X 20CM (6 X 8IN)
FELT FOR THE DRESS

SCRAPS OF
FELT FOR THE
FLOWER PETALS

15 X 25CM (6 X 10IN) FELT
FOR THE INNER LINING
OF THE CAPE

15 X 15CM
(6 X 6IN) FELT
FOR THE
BLOUSE

15 X 25CM
(6 X 10IN) FELT FOR
THE OUTER CAPE

BRUSHED
MOHAIR
WOOL FOR
THE HAIR

CRAFT FLOWER
STAMENS,
FOUND IN CAKE
DECORATING
SECTION

SCRAP OF FELT
FOR THE BOW

7.5 X 15CM
(3 X 6IN)
FELT FOR
THE INNER
BONNET EAR

CUTTING AND ASSEMBLY

1 Follow the steps for making the Basic Doll up to Step 10 of the Hair section (see How to Sew the Basic Doll).

HAIR

1 To style the doll's hair, simply gather it all at the back of the head and tie together with a narrow ribbon.

BONNET

1 Using your disappearing ink marker, first transfer all the dots, the X marking and the ruled lines shown on the bonnet gusset and side patterns onto the felt pieces you have cut for them.

2 Align dot A on one felt side piece with dot A on the bonnet gusset, wrong sides facing, and pin a couple of times along the top edge (see **Fig A**).

3 Align dot B on the side piece with dot B on the gusset. Then whip stitch (see Stitch Guide) the curved outer edge of the bonnet side to the edge of the bonnet gusset from A to B (see **Fig A**). Repeat for the opposite side.

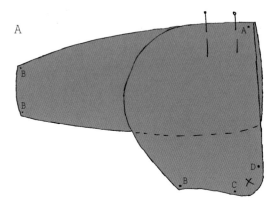

4 Follow Steps 1 to 3 to make the inner lining for the bonnet.

5 Turn the inner lining so the wrong side of the felt is facing outwards. Tuck the inner lining into the outer bonnet, gently pushing it all the way back and aligning the seams that run down on either side (see **Fig B**).

Then pin the edges of the lining to the edges of the outer bonnet.

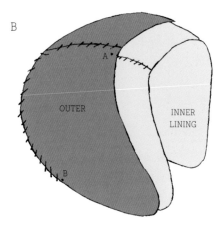

6 Double thread a needle with embroidery thread (floss) in a contrasting shade to the lining. Then blanket stitch (see Stitch Guide) around the opening of the bonnet, beginning at one of the seams at B on the back nape edge and stitching around the bottom of the bonnet until you reach the dot marked C (see **Fig C**).

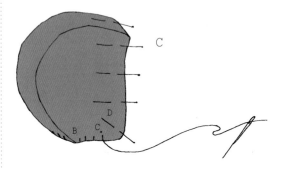

7 Gently open the area between C and D then position the end of an 18cm (7in) length of seam binding onto the X marking. Pin this in place, inserting the pin from the inside of the bonnet lining so that you can easily remove it once the seam binding is stitched in place (see **Fig D**).

8 Pin the edges of the bonnet between C and D, then carry on blanket stitching around the front edge of the bonnet until you reach dots C and D on the opposite side.

9 Now insert the seam binding on this side, as you did in Step 7, pinning it in place on the X marking between dots C and D (see **Fig D**).

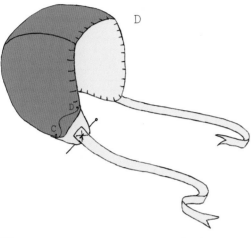

10 Pin the bonnet edges between C and D then carry on blanket stitching around the bottom edge of the bonnet until you reach the spot you started at. End off your thread.

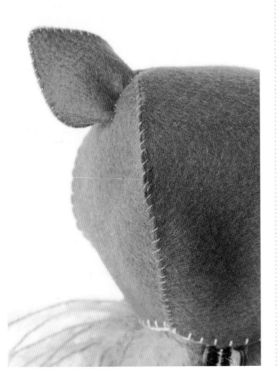

DEER EARS

1 Using your disappearing ink marker, first transfer the dots marked A, B, C and D shown on the deer ear patterns onto the felt pieces you have cut for them.

2 To make one ear, position the inner felt ear onto the outer one, wrong sides facing. Pin these together then whip stitch around the top outer edges from A to B (see **Fig E**).

3 Fold the bottom corner of the ear so the dot marked B aligns with dot D, then blanket stitch the bottom edge down. Fold the other bottom corner of the ear, so that the dot marked A aligns with dot C, then blanket stitch this bottom edge down too (see **Fig F**).

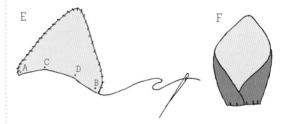

4 Now pin the base of the ear onto the marked area on the side of the bonnet. Ladder stitch (see Stitch Guide) the front and back of the ear in place (see **Fig G**). If the ear still feels a little wobbly, ladder stitch around it once more to anchor it in place.

5 Repeat Steps 2 to 4 to complete the other ear (see **Fig G**).

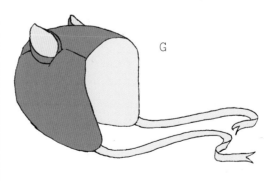

CAPE

1 Using your disappearing ink marker, first transfer all the dots and ruled lines shown on the cape patterns onto the felt pieces you have cut for it.

2 Using your marked lines as guides, position the pieces of felt you have cut for the faux pocket between the dotted lines on the right side of the felt piece for the outer cape. Then appliqué stitch (see Stitch Guide) around the pockets, leaving the long edge at the back side of the pocket open to give the illusion of a functioning pocket.

3 Now whip stitch the darts on either side of the outer cape together, making sure you stitch them from the wrong side of the felt, then gently open each one out and smooth (see **Fig H**). Repeat the process for the darts on the felt piece for the inner lining.

H

4 Position the inner lining on top of the outer cape, wrong sides facing, aligning at the darts. Pin the edges of both pieces together.

5 Blanket stitch around the outer edges of the cape, sewing from dot A with double embroidery thread in a contrasting shade that matches the lining, and work around to the opposite side at B. Do not blanket stitch around the neck edge and do not end off your thread yet (see **Fig I**).

I

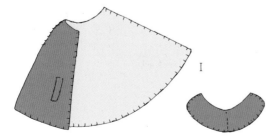

6 Now blanket stitch the outer edge of the collar from A to B (see **Fig I**).

7 Position the collar onto the cape, aligning dots A, B and C on the collar with dots A, B and C on the cape, then pin in place. Blanket stitch the collar to the cape's neck edge, using the thread left over from Step 5 (see **Fig J**).

8 Sew the hook and eye closure on either side of the cape, just below the edge of the neck at the front (see **Fig J**).

J

BLOUSE

1 Using your disappearing ink marker, first transfer all the dots shown on the blouse pattern onto the felt pieces you have cut for it.

2 Fold the blouse in half at the shoulder, wrong sides facing. Whip stitch the side seams together, starting at the dot below each armhole and working down to the dot at the hem (see **Fig K**).

3 Now blanket stitch around the entire neck opening, as well as the bottom edge and armholes of the blouse (see **Fig L**). This will reinforce these openings and prevent them from warping while you are dressing the doll.

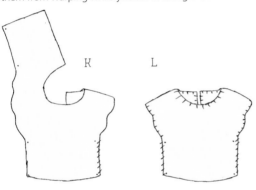

4 Finally sew a snap closure on either side of the blouse back, just below the neckline.

DRESS

1 Using your disappearing ink marker, first transfer all the dots, X markings and ruled lines shown on the dress patterns onto the felt pieces you have cut for it. Then, using your markings as a guide, embroider the details at the hem of the dress.

2 Using one strand of embroidery thread, blanket stitch around the top edge of the dress from dot A to dot B on the opposite side (see **Fig M**). Do not end off your thread yet.

3 Again using your markings as a guide, embroider the details onto the pocket then position it in place. Appliqué stitch three edges of the pocket onto the dress, leaving the top edge open (see **Fig M**).

4 Sew female snap closures onto the X markings at the front of the dress (see **Fig M**).

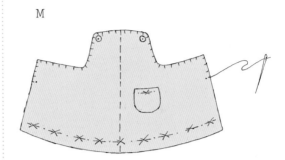

5 Fold the dress so that the sides join at the back. Using the leftover thread from Step 2, whip stitch these sides together, starting at dots A and B and working down. Then stitch a snap closure at the top of the back seam (see **Fig N**).

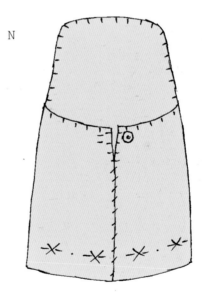

6 For the shoulder straps, blanket stitch around the edges of the two pieces of felt you have cut for the straps. Sew a male snap closure at one end of each strap, on the wrong side of the felt (see **Fig O**).

7 Turn the straps over so that the right sides are facing you then carefully sew a tiny button onto the area above the male snap closure (see **Fig O**).

O

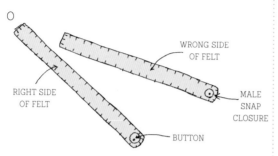

WRONG SIDE OF FELT

RIGHT SIDE OF FELT

MALE SNAP CLOSURE

BUTTON

8 Fit the dress onto the doll. Connect the male snap closures on the shoulder straps to the female ones at the front of the dress, then turn the doll so that her back is facing you. Position the straps over her shoulders, crossing them at the back of her body. Tuck the ends of the straps into the dress, carefully pinning them in place as shown (see **Fig P**).

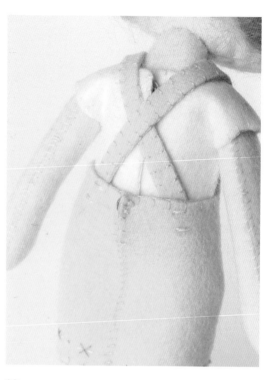

P

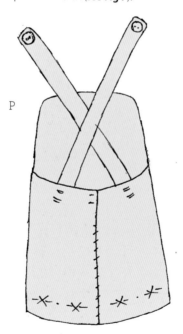

9 Open the snap closures at the front of the dress then gently slide the dress off the doll. Stitch the straps into place at the back of the dress.

10 To finish, cut a length of lace trim to fit around the hem. Apply a small bead of Fray Check liquid to both ends and allow it to dry thoroughly. Then pin the lace trim to the hem and use tiny straight stitches to sew it in place (see **Fig Q**).

Q

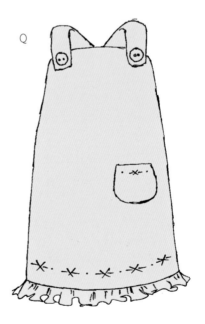

4 Fold the sock in half lengthways, right sides facing, and pin. Back stitch around the sock, about 4mm (⅛in) away from the edge, starting at the dot at the top of the folded edge and working down to the dot at the toe (see **Fig S**). Then turn this sock the right side out.

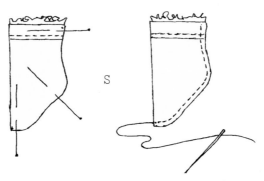

S

5 Repeat Steps 1 to 4 to complete the other sock.

SOCKS

1 Using your disappearing ink marker, first transfer the fold line and dots shown on the sock pattern onto the two felt pieces you have cut for them.

2 To make one sock, fold the top edge over towards the wrong side of the fabric, following the guideline, then iron this flat.

3 Now turn the sock over so that the right side of the fabric is facing you. Cut a length of lace trim to fit across the top edge, apply a small bead of Fray Check liquid to both ends and allow to dry thoroughly. Then pin the lace trim along the top edge of the sock and back stitch (see Stitch Guide) this in place (see **Fig R**).

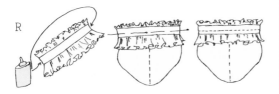

R

SHOES

1 Using your disappearing ink marker, first transfer the dots and the ruled lines shown on the shoe top and sole patterns onto the felt pieces you have cut for them.

2 To make one shoe, use a contrasting embroidery thread to blanket stitch around the inner cut-out centre and the inner edge of the shoe top (see **Fig T**).

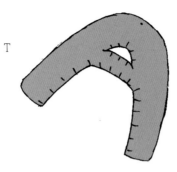

T

3 Now fold the shoe top in half and whip stitch the back ends together (see **Fig U**).

U

4 Place the felt sole piece onto the bottom of the shoe top, aligning the dots at the heel and toe, then blanket stitch them together (see **Fig V**).

V

5 Repeat Steps 1 to 4 to complete the other shoe.

BASKET

1 Using your disappearing ink marker, first transfer the X marking on side A of the basket pattern onto the two felt pieces you have cut for this.

2 Now embroider tiny flowers and leaves onto one side of both pieces of felt you have cut for side B. For each of the flowers, use a different colour thread and the lazy daisy stitch (see Stitch Guide); for each of the leaves, use green thread and embroider one 'petal' of the lazy daisy flower.

3 Whip stitch the short bottom edges of both sides A to the short edges of the basket base. Then whip stitch the short bottom edges of both sides B to the long sides of the basket base (see **Fig W**).

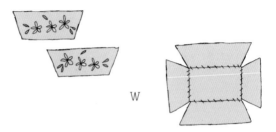

W

4 Whip stitch the edges of sides A to sides B then repeat the process with the felt pieces for the basket liner. You'll now have two basket bases; the slightly smaller liner will be inserted into the larger outer basket in Step 7 to help make the basket sturdier (see **Fig X**).

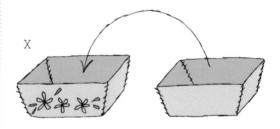

X

5 Fold the felt piece for the basket handle in half lengthways, pin this in place, then blanket stitch the edges together. Now flatten the handle so the blanket stitches are running down the centre and blanket stitch the short edges on either side together (see **Fig Y**).

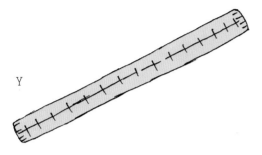

Y

6 Position one short end of the basket handle onto the inside of one side A, aligning it with the X marked near the top centre of this side, and pin in place. Using small stitches, sew the handle end onto the inside of the short side of the basket, then repeat this process on the opposite side (see **Fig Z**).

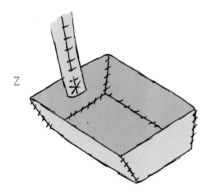

Z

7 Tuck the liner into the outer basket, making sure that the short and long sides of both match up, and that the top edges align. Then blanket stitch around the entire top edge with contrasting embroidery thread to fix the lining in place, being careful to stitch through the basket handle at each end too (see **Fig AA**).

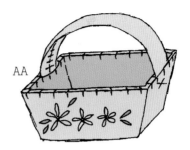

AA

FLOWERS

1 To make one little flower, cut a flower stamen to measure 3cm (1¼in) in length. If your stamens are white, use a green felt pen to colour them.

2 Make a little dot in the centre of the piece of felt you have cut for the flower with a contrasting felt marker. Now insert the tip of an awl into the centre, pushing it through until there's an opening large enough to insert the cut end of the flower stamen.

3 Cut as many petals and stamens as you'd like then repeat Steps 1 to 2, inserting the cut end of each stamen into the centre of each flower petal as you go (see **Fig BB**).

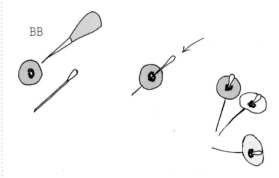

BB

4 Appliqué stitch the curved edge of the body onto the head. Stitch a seed bead onto the area marked for the eye then add a tiny eyelash to the outer edge and a tiny eyebrow above each eye (see **Fig DD**).

DD

5 Pin the sides of the hedgehog together, wrong sides facing. Beginning at the neck and using embroidery thread that matches the head, whip stitch around the head (see **Fig EE**).

EE

6 Now, using embroidery thread that matches the body colour, blanket stitch around the body, starting where the body meets the top of the head and stopping at the dot at the bottom of the back.

7 Insert tiny pinches of stuffing, using a cocktail (orange) stick to gently push this into the snout area. Once the snout is filled continue adding stuffing to the head, using the cocktail stick to carefully push in the stuffing to round it out.

HEDGEHOG

1 Using your disappearing ink pen, transfer the markings for the quills onto the felt body pieces, and add the eye, eyebrow markings and dots at the forehead and neck onto the felt pieces for the head. Then use your pink pencil to colour in the lower area of the ears.

2 Embroider quills onto each body piece using double embroidery thread (see **Fig CC**) – I used two different colours together to create an interesting effect.

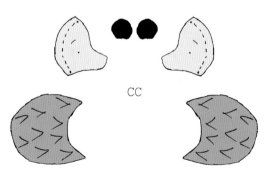

CC

3 Position each body piece onto the corresponding piece of the head, aligning the curved edges of the body with the dots at the forehead and neck, then pin in place.

8 Thread a needle with pink embroidery thread and insert it through the opening at the base of the hedgehog's body and out through one side of the top of the snout. Using tiny satin stitches (see Stitch Guide), embroider a tiny nose in place then end off the thread (see **Fig FF**).

FF

9 Now add stuffing to round out the body then continue blanket stitching around the base of the body to close the hole.

10 Fold each ear in half and make a couple of tiny blanket stitches along their bases to hold them in this shape (see **Fig GG**). Do not end off your thread, as you'll use it to stitch the ears onto the head.

GG

11 Insert a pin into the base of each ear and position them on either side of the head, taking time to ensure that they are both evenly spaced and facing forwards (see **Fig HH**). Once you are satisfied with the placement, ladder stitch the front and back of each ear onto the head.

HH

12 Position the piece of felt you have cut for the bow just below an ear, pinning it in place (see **Fig II**). Insert a threaded needle up through the area between the neck and body and out, just off-centre in the middle of the bow. Make a tiny stitch, taking your needle out again through the area between the neck and body, then end off your thread.

13 Finally, use your pink pencil to add a bit of colour to the cheek area then fit the hedgehog into the basket, along with some flowers (see **Fig II**).

II

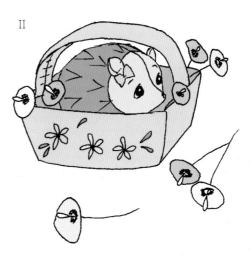

PATTERNS
Woodland Maiden

Also use the patterns from the Basic Doll project (see How to Sew the Basic Doll).
All the patterns are actual size, so there is no need to enlarge or reduce them.

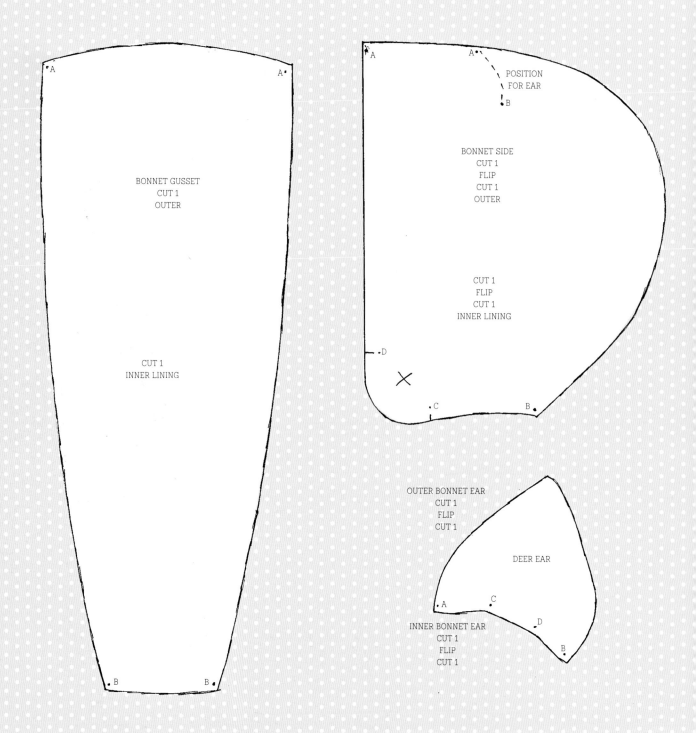

A

A

BONNET GUSSET
CUT 1
OUTER

CUT 1
INNER LINING

B   B

A

A

POSITION
FOR EAR

B

BONNET SIDE
CUT 1
FLIP
CUT 1
OUTER

CUT 1
FLIP
CUT 1
INNER LINING

D

C   B

OUTER BONNET EAR
CUT 1
FLIP
CUT 1

DEER EAR

A   C

D

INNER BONNET EAR
CUT 1
FLIP
CUT 1

B

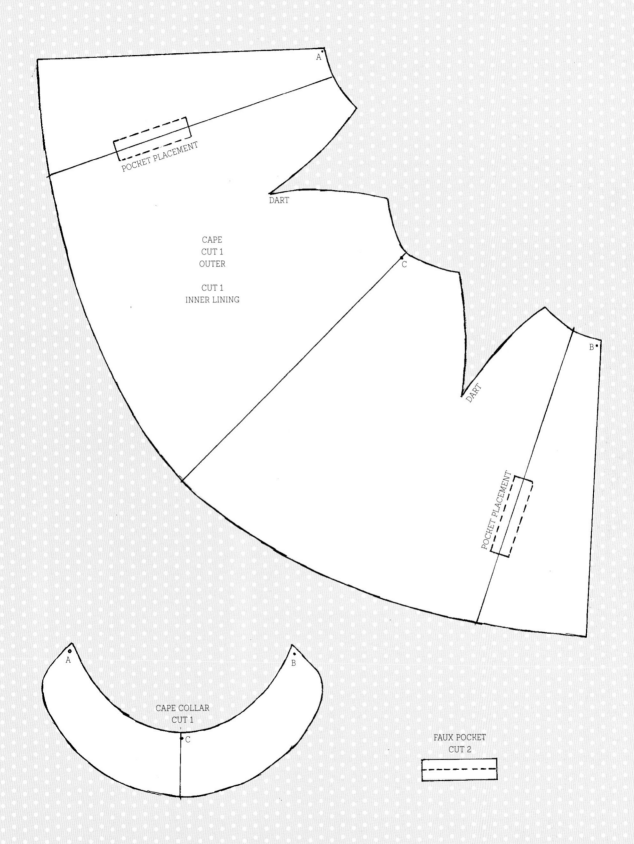

POCKET PLACEMENT

A

DART

CAPE
CUT 1
OUTER

CUT 1
INNER LINING

C

B

DART

POCKET PLACEMENT

A

B

CAPE COLLAR
CUT 1

C

FAUX POCKET
CUT 2

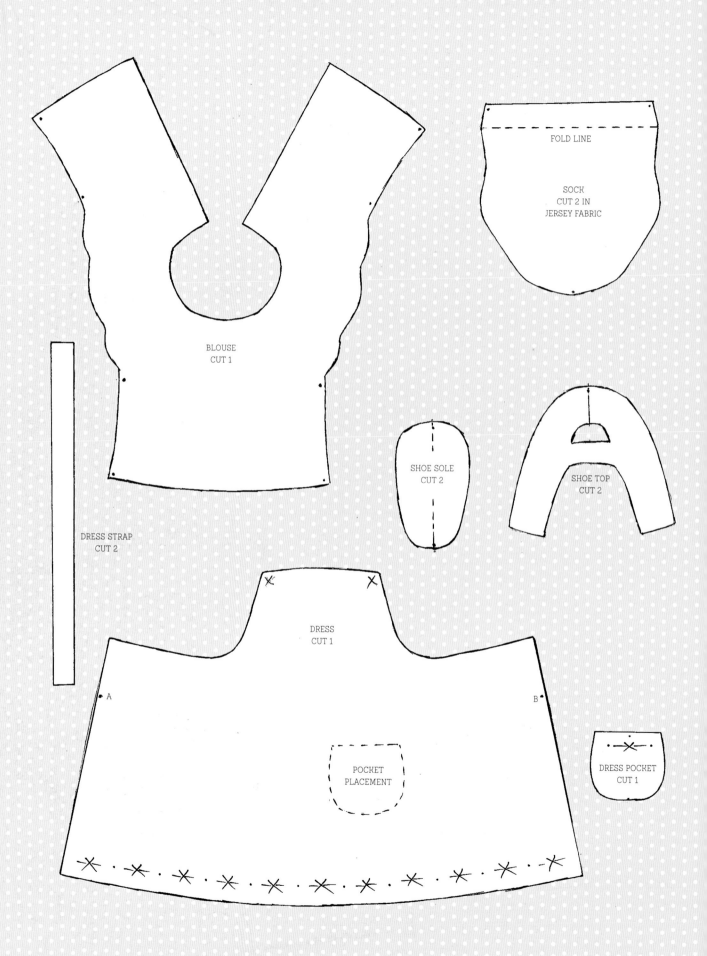

FOLD LINE

SOCK
CUT 2 IN
JERSEY FABRIC

BLOUSE
CUT 1

SHOE SOLE
CUT 2

SHOE TOP
CUT 2

DRESS STRAP
CUT 2

DRESS
CUT 1

A

B

POCKET
PLACEMENT

DRESS POCKET
CUT 1

BASKET HANDLE
CUT 1

FLOWER
CUT AS MANY AS
NEEDED

BASKET BASE
CUT 1

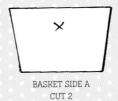

BASKET SIDE A
CUT 2

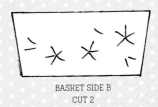

BASKET SIDE B
CUT 2

BASKET BASE LINER
CUT 1

BASKET SIDE A LINER
CUT 2

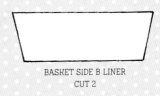

BASKET SIDE B LINER
CUT 2

HEDGEHOG'S BOW
CUT 1

HEDGEHOG'S EAR
CUT 2

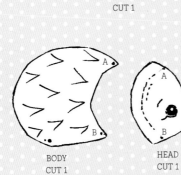

BODY
CUT 1

HEAD
CUT 1

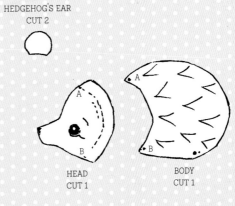

HEAD
CUT 1

BODY
CUT 1

PERSONALIZING
Your Doll

THERE ARE ENDLESS WAYS TO CREATE A PERSONALIZED DOLL, ESPECIALLY IF YOU'RE MAKING IT AS A GIFT FOR SOMEONE SPECIAL. USE THE IDEAS I'VE PROVIDED HERE AS INSPIRATION TO GET YOU STARTED WITH THIS, OR BECOME CREATIVE YOURSELF, THINKING UP SOME FABULOUS WAYS TO CUSTOMIZE YOUR OWN LITTLE DOLLS FOR YOUR FRIENDS AND FAMILY.

PERSONALIZING THE HAIR

Consider choosing a wool (yarn) to match the colour of the recipient's hair, or consider matching the texture, perhaps using a bouclé yarn to create a curly appearance or an Icelandic wool with its course and wavier texture. I've provided details of the wool or wool blends and colours I used for the projects in the box opposite (see Wools (yarns) Used for Hair in the Projects), but you can choose any wool you like for your own creations.

You will also find ideas throughout the book for creating different hairstyles. Once your little doll is complete and the glue on the back of its head has thoroughly dried, the hair can be carefully trimmed at the ends, or it can be cut quite short, similar to the style I created for the Circus Ringmaster project (see Circus Ringmaster). It's best to cut the hair while the doll is still wearing his or her birthday suit to avoid bits of wool falling on the clothing.

Here are some examples of the different colours and textures you can use for your own dolls.

To cut the hair, first gather up the loose strands from the top bundle then fix these up and out of the way. You'll be left with the layer of hair that has been glued onto the head. Place a piece of paper towel on the doll's back, underneath this layer of hair, so that the bits cut off don't end up on the skin. Determine how short you'd like to go then carefully trim, starting at the centre back and working out to each side. Arrange the top layer over the bottom layer and cut it to match.

To create a fringe, cut one strand at a time, starting at the centre area between the eyebrows and working outwards to the sides. Try to avoid tugging on the strands while you're cutting, as these can subsequently spring up and be shorter than you intended. To finish, you might like to use tiny hair barrettes, clamps and pretty ribbons to style the hair.

Follow the simple instructions above to trim your dolls' hair and fringes.

WOOLS (YARNS) USED FOR HAIR IN THE PROJECTS

Prima Ballerina	Lett-Lopi Lite	(Straw, Number 1418)
Circus Ringmaster, Beach Babe	Lett-Lopi Lite	(Black, Number 0059)
Girls' Night Out	Lett-Lopi Lite	(Camel, Number 1400)
Cute Schoolgirl	Louisa Harding Grace	(Savon, Number 052)
Little Princess	Juniper Moon Farm Moonshine	(Conch Shell, Number 003)
Flower Fairy	Juey BFL Ice Cream DK	(Lavender, Number 06)
Little Mermaid (pink)	Blue Sky Alpacas Brushed Suri	(Pink Lémonade, Number 907)
Bedtime Doll	Wendy Aspire	(Vapor, Number 3243)
Little Traveller	Freia Fibers Hand Dyed Gradient Yarn	(Pixie Ombre)
Woodland Maiden	Mohair Smooth Waldorf Doll Yarn	(Ginger)

PERSONALIZING THE SKIN AND EYE COLOUR

—

You may also want to consider personalizing the skin and eye colour of the doll you're making, as well as the hair. There are plenty of felts available in different skin colours, and I've used a few different ones for the dolls throughout this book. Meanwhile, safety eyes are available in a wide range of colours and can easily be matched to the eye colour of the recipient.

Here are some examples of different skin tones you may wish to consider for your own dolls, ranging from sun-kissed tan to golden caramel, and peaches and cream to pale porcelain.

PERSONALIZING THE OUTFITS

Many of the outfits from the different themes in the book can be mixed and matched to create completely new outfits altogether. For example, you could pair the little skirt from the Cute Schoolgirl project (see Cute Schoolgirl) with any of the tops from the Little Princess (see Little Princess), Woodland Maiden (see Woodland Maiden), or Bedtime Doll (see Bedtime Doll) projects to create a sweet little summer outfit.

Then the big floppy hat from the Beach Babe project (see Beach Babe) would look lovely paired with the Little Traveller's dress (see Little Traveller) to create the perfect outfit for an afternoon tea party. Meanwhile the trousers from the Circus Ringmaster's outfit (see Circus Ringmaster) could be made with a patterned or coloured felt then paired with any of the tops to create a completely new look.

Another idea is to create an outfit for a sports lover. By omitting the lace trim on the pyjama top and bottoms (see Bedtime Doll), you could easily transform this outfit into a sports uniform to match the colours of the team. Embroidering the name of the player or team onto the top would add a lovely personal touch.

Create an outfit for a sports lover by customizing the pyjamas shown in the projects.

Mix and match items from the projects to create completely new looks, as I've done here.

STITCH Guide

ALL OF THE PROJECTS IN THIS BOOK ARE DESIGNED TO BE SEWN BY HAND, USING BASIC STITCHES AS WELL AS SOME EASY EMBROIDERY STITCHES, AS SPECIFIED IN THE PROJECT INSTRUCTIONS. IF YOU'VE NEVER HAND STITCHED OR EMBROIDERED BEFORE, I RECOMMEND THAT YOU PRACTISE EACH STITCH ON A SCRAP PIECE OF FELT – PLEASE REMEMBER TO KEEP YOUR STITCHES SMALL, NEAT AND EVENLY SPACED TO ENSURE A NICE CLEAN FINISH AND TO PREVENT ANY STUFFING ESCAPING FROM THE SEAMS. ONCE YOU FEEL CONFIDENT IN YOUR ABILITY TO STITCH, YOU CAN BEGIN MAKING THE LITTLE DOLLS AND THEIR OUTFITS.

This is a simple linear stitch mostly used to decorate fabric edges. Bring your threaded needle out through A, insert the needle at B and bring it out again at C. Keeping the thread under the needle, pull it gently so that it is taut, forming a right angle. To continue, insert the needle at D, keeping the thread under the needle as you bring it out at E.

This is a basic stitch used to sew two edges of felt together. Insert the needle through the wrong side of one piece of felt, then out through the right side at A. Now insert the needle through the wrong side of the other piece of felt at B, taking it through both felt layers and out through the opposite side at C. Continue in this manner, sewing both edges of felt together.

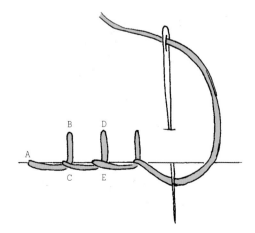

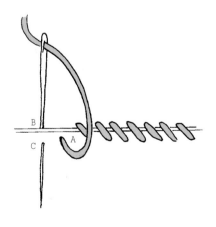

LADDER Stitch

The ladder stitch, also called the blind or hidden stitch, is mainly used to close an opening or to join two sections, such as the head and the body. The stitch is worked back and forth along the edges of the head and neck where they meet, catching a tiny bit of each side as it goes. When pulled tight, the thread will create an invisible seam to attach the head onto the neck of the body. To stitch, bring your needle out through A, insert the needle at B then out through C, insert the needle at D then out through E, and so on. Every now and then gently pull the thread taut, as this will make the stitches disappear. Remember to keep your stitches tiny, straight and even as you work.

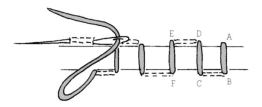

Tip

TRY NOT TO PULL YOUR LADDER STITCHES TOO TIGHTLY, AS THIS WILL CAUSE THE SEAM BETWEEN THE HEAD AND NECK YOU ARE SEWING TO LOOK PUCKERED.

STEM Stitch

The stem stitch, also known as the outline stitch, produces a slightly raised, solid line that is perfect for outlining curves, such as the lips and nose of the doll. Bring your needle out through A then insert the needle at B, holding the thread down with your thumb, then come up through C, halfway between A and B. Release the thread under your thumb and gently pull it taut. Repeat, keeping your stitches small and neat.

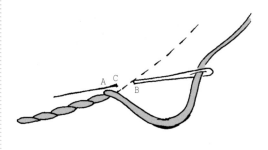

BACK Stitch

A similar stitch to stem stitch, making a finer, slightly raised line that is good for outlines and details. Bring your threaded needle up through A and insert at B to make a straight stitch. Bring your needle back through at C and go down again at A to make a second straight stitch. Bring your needle up a stitch length ahead of C, then insert down at C, and so on.

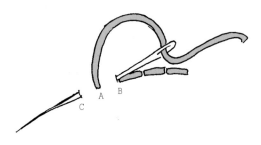

APPLIQUÉ Stitch

Appliqué stitch is usually used to attach a smaller piece of felt onto a larger one. First position the small piece in place then insert the needle through the back of the felt at A. Stitch down into B, through again at C, and so on until you've stitched the smaller piece into place.

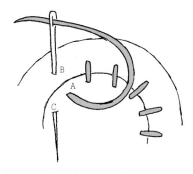

STRAIGHT, GATHERING AND RUNNING Stitches

These stitches are all made using the same basic technique, and should all be of an even length, as should the spaces between them. Basic straight stitches can be used to make little eyelashes or eyebrows; running stitches are usually made along a straight or curved line with even spaces between the stitches; and gathering stitches are made in the same manner as running stitches, but the thread is pulled firmly to create a gathered effect on the fabric, ribbon, seam binding or trim. Insert the threaded needle through the back of the fabric at A then insert the needle down into the fabric at B. Bring the needle back up a stitch length ahead of B and insert again at C, and so forth.

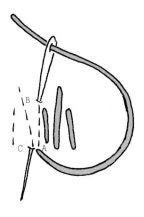

SATIN *Stitch*

Satin stitch is mostly used to fill in an area, similar to colouring within the lines of a children's colouring book. A basic satin stitch is made by working straight stitches close together in parallel lines, and although the technique is simple, it is helpful to practise it a few times to achieve perfect results. Bring your threaded needle up through A, insert into B, come through again at C, and so on until you've filled the area. It's important to keep the tension even throughout, as this will create a smooth satin look to the stitched area.

LAZY DAISY *Stitch*

Also called detached chain stitch, this is an isolated stitch that is usually worked around in a circle to create the appearance of flower petals, and used singularly, it can be used to create little leaves. Bring the needle through to the front of the fabric at the top of the dotted line at A. Insert the needle right back into A and bring it out through the front at B, looping the thread under the needle point, then pull the thread so that the loop lies flat. Make a very short stitch over the loop and insert the needle down at C to anchor it. Bring the needle out through to the top of the next marked line at A and repeat the process, working around until you've completed the flower.

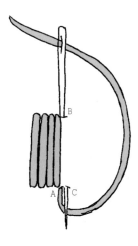

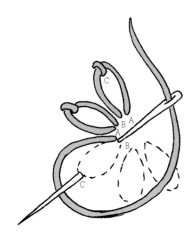

Tip

TRY TO KEEP YOUR SATIN
STITCHES AS CLOSE
TOGETHER AS POSSIBLE
WITHOUT OVERLAPPING
THEM AND WITHOUT
LEAVING SPACES BETWEEN
EACH STITCH.

ACKNOWLEDGMENTS

Special thanks to everyone at FW Media who contributed to the making of this book
– this wonderful adventure would not have been possible without your help and
guidance. In particular, I'd like to thank Ame Verso for first contacting me with the
idea for the book, Freya Dangerfield for the fabulous job she's done editing the book,
and Debbie Jackson and Jane Trollope for their encouragement along the way.

Many thanks to Mom for all your help, your cutting skills are extraordinary! Thank you, too, to
my two favourite 'critique-ers', my two boys Jody and Dylan – you have both been so good at
offering your opinions when I've asked for them, and I'm so grateful for your encouragement!

I'd like to dedicate this book to my wonderful husband John, whose help on every level
has been invaluable. Without you this would not have been possible, so thank you!

ABOUT THE AUTHOR

I live in beautiful British Columbia, Canada, in the pretty historical city of New Westminster,
with my hubby of 21 years and our two grown boys. Our sunny flat overlooks the
Fraser River and the Strait of Georgia, beyond which we can see the mountain ranges
on Vancouver Island. My 'studio' is really a tiny corner in our dining room, filled with
stacks of felt, pattern pieces, odd buttons and bits and pieces of trim. I love collecting old
children's books filled with fairytales and nursery rhymes, and I'm very fond of Japanese
Shojo manga art, especially vintage illustrations from the 1950s, 60s and 70s.

SUPPLIERS

MOST OF THE SUPPLIES AND MATERIALS NEEDED TO
MAKE THE PROJECTS IN THIS BOOK CAN BE SOURCED
AT FABRIC, YARN AND CRAFT STORES. THERE ARE
ALSO MANY ONLINE SUPPLIERS IF YOU'RE UNABLE TO
FIND WHAT YOU NEED LOCALLY.

GINGERMELON DOLLS

www.etsy.com/ca/shop/Gingermelon

My Etsy shop, where you can find doll and toy patterns
and pattern kits created by me. I also offer a large
selection of pure merino wool felts, wool blend felts,
printed felts, and other supplies such as safety eyes, tiny
buttons, seam bindings and felting needles.

STITCH CRAFT CREATE

www.stitchcraftcreate.co.uk

Crafters' heaven! Here you'll find a large selection of
crafty products, from fabrics and wools (yarns) to craft
books and patterns. There's also a wonderful section
filled with ideas and free projects.

ETSY

www.etsy.com

This is an online marketplace where artists can sell their
handmade goods, and it's a great place for finding
supplies and fabrics, too.

MICHAELS

www.michaels.com

Stocks embroidery threads, stuffing, craft glue, glitter,
seed beads, buttons and so on.

LOVEKNITTING

loveknitting.com

Find wool, patterns, knitting needles, books and
accessories here.

DERAMORES

www.deramores.com

Wool, patterns, knitting needles, books and accessories.

BLACK SHEEP YARNS

blacksheepyarns.ca

Wool, accessories, books and patterns.

ALAFOSS

www.alafoss.is

This site stocks Icelandic wool.

INDEX

A DAVID & CHARLES BOOK
© F&W Media International, Ltd 2015

David & Charles is an imprint of F&W Media International, Ltd
Brunel House, Forde Close, Newton Abbot, TQ12 4PU, UK

F&W Media International, Ltd is a subsidiary of F+W Media, Inc
10151 Carver Road, Suite #200, Blue Ash, OH 45242, USA

Text and Designs © Michelle Down
Layout and Photography © F&W Media International, Ltd 2015

First published in the UK and USA in 2015
Michelle Down has asserted her right to be identified as author of this work in accordance
with the Copyright, Designs and Patents Act, 1988.

A catalogue record for this book is available from the British Library.

ISBN-13: 978-1-4463-0576-8 paperback
ISBN-10: 1-4463-0576-7 paperback

ISBN-13: 978-1-4463-7100-8 PDF
ISBN-10: 1-4463-7100-X PDF

ISBN-13: 978-1-4463-7099-5 EPUB
ISBN-10: 1-4463-7099-2 EPUB

Printed in China by RR Donnelley for:
F&W Media International, Ltd
Brunel House, Forde Close, Newton Abbot, TQ12 4PU, UK

10 9 8 7 6 5 4 3 2 1

Acquisitions Editor Ame Verso
Managing Editor Honor Head
Desk Editor Jane Trollope
Project Editor Freya Dangerfield
Designer Prudence Rogers
Photographer Jason Jenkins
Production Controller Beverley Richardson

F+W Media publishes high quality books on a wide range of subjects.
For more great book ideas visit: www.stitchcraftcreate.co.uk

Layout of the digital edition of this book may vary depending on reader
hardware and display settings.